BRICKER OF OHIO:

THE MAN AND HIS RECORD

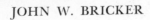

JOHN W. BRICKER

BRICKER OF OHIO

THE MAN AND HIS RECORD

By KARL B. PAULY

FOUNDED 1838
GPPS

G. P. PUTNAM'S SONS
NEW YORK

PREFACE

THIS BOOK was written to give the people of the United States detailed information about one of the outstanding candidates for the Republican presidential nomination. Even the most extended campaign, with all the modern devices of communication, cannot give all the people of the country an opportunity to hear the whole story of any man's life and record. This year there are American voters in every section of the globe, and Congress and the states are trying to shape the nation's election machinery to reach them all with ballots.

Believing that the people want to know about a man who deserves their consideration for the highest office at their disposal much more than the man himself can tell them in the most vigorous campaign, I have gathered together from the records of the various state departments, from official papers and correspondence, and from the newspapers the whole story of Governor Bricker's record in office, what he has done already for the state of Ohio. I have drawn, too, from my personal, close-hand observations of John Bricker during the nineteen years I have known him. When I first met him, he was just starting his career in the government service; I have watched him grow, observed all of his campaigns for public office and his achievements in those offices. I have tried to show also what went into the making of the man who accomplished what Bricker has done—giving enough of his personal story to show the kind of person he is, how he lives and what his personal tastes are. These things, too, people want to know about a man who may have their national destiny in his hands.

Karl B. Pauly

Columbus, Ohio
January 15, 1944

vi

CONTENTS

ILLUSTRATIONS

    viii

BRICKER OF OHIO:

THE MAN AND HIS RECORD

CHAPTER I

"BRICKER FOR PRESIDENT"

IT WAS ONLY to be expected that John Bricker should be mentioned for President of the United States soon after his election as governor of Ohio. Historical, geographical, and political precedents alone would have made him a presidential possibility, but in Bricker's case there were more than traditional reasons. His election in 1938 marked the resurgence of the Republican party in the nation. He led his ticket; he had the party in his state solidly behind him; he had spoken out emphatically on controversial issues and attracted thousands of independent votes. He was a man with a record, and beyond doubt a man with a future.

Ohio is called "Mother of Presidents" not without reason. Seven Presidents have been natives of the state, and an eighth lived there at the time of his election—a record no other state can equal. No mere coincidence accounts for the number of Presidents Ohio has produced; it is a natural consequence of her geographical and political situation in respect to the nation as a whole.

In the first place, Ohio is a cross section of the na-

3

tion. She stands fourth in population, with typical proportions of Negroes, foreign-born, and native Americans; third in the pay rolls of industry; fifth in agriculture; and fifth in value of manufactured products. Ohio is neither predominantly agricultural nor predominantly industrial, but huge and diversified farm production marches side by side with huge and diversified factory production. On the one hand, she ranks fifth among the states in production of wheat; on the other, she is third in production of coal, and fourth in petroleum production. Two-fifths of her people live in cities of 100,000 or more, the rest in small towns and rural areas.

Geographically, Ohio is the crossroads of the nation. There the East ends and the West begins, and all main east-west trunk lines cross the state. She has more than 200 miles of Lake Erie shoreline and some of the largest inland ports of the world. Four hundred miles of canalized Ohio River flow along her eastern and southern boundaries, bearing commerce to and from the heart of the nation. This central position, her direct commercial contacts, and her representative population remove from Ohio all taint of sectionalism.

In presidential nominating conventions Ohio has the fourth largest block of votes among all states, both in the convention and in the electoral college. More than that, she is pivotal; and the swinging pivot is a weathervane. In the last twelve presidential elections, Ohio has unerringly given her electoral vote to the winning candidate, seven times to a Republican and five to a Democrat. That record, too, no other state can match.

Bricker's election to the governorship of this cross-section state was no political accident. The people who chose him had been watching him for ten years, during which he had established a record of honesty, fair-dealing, soundness, vision, and exceptional administrative ability. When they wanted someone to bring order and security out of confusion, mismanagement, and chicanery in public affairs, it was to Bricker they turned. Since 1938 they have been confirmed in the wisdom of their choice and have re-elected him twice, each time by a larger majority.

In 1938 Bricker's majority was 118,225; in 1940 it more than tripled, to 364,467. That year he received 1,824,863 votes, the largest number ever received by any candidate for any office in the history of Ohio. In 1942 his majority went still higher, to 377,338.

During these years his popularity has increased over wider areas as well as numerically. Originally strongest in rural districts, it is now equally great in industrial counties. In his first two victories, Bricker carried 77 out of the 88 counties; in the 1942 election he had all but two counties. In 1938 he carried 8 of the 11 counties having a population of over 100,000; but, combined, he lost them by 20,793. Two years later he carried 9 of these 11 largest counties by a combined majority of 182,536. In 1942 he carried all 11 by a majority of 154,713. Cleveland, Cincinnati, Columbus, Toledo, Akron, Youngstown, Dayton, Springfield, Canton, Warren, Massillon, Niles, Hamilton, Middletown, Lorain, and Elyria all are embraced within these 11 counties.

Of 16 counties with a population of between 50,000 and 100,000, he carried 13 in 1938 and 1940, and all of them in 1942. In this middle bracket of counties his majority has increased each time—from 39,086 in 1938, to 43,715 in 1940, to 64,432 in 1942.

In 1938 Bricker carried 56 of the 61 rural counties; 55 in 1940; and 59 in 1942, losing only Holmes and Pike, the two most traditionally rockbound Democratic counties in the state. His rural majority rose from 99,936 in 1938, to 138,216 in 1940, to 158,193 in 1942.

No other governor of Ohio has ever received such widespread approval of the voters. The reasons for Bricker's popularity are simple: he has given Ohio sound, orderly, economical government; and he has given the people of his state militant leadership in their desire to keep the American form of government, with its division of powers and its reliance on democratic processes while moving in orderly fashion toward improved social and economic conditions. The people of Ohio believe with their governor that "no superman or dictator can point the way to the better life we seek. It is a democratic task. The leadership must be of the many, of people of high character and good purpose. Such leadership is undramatic but safe. By it, democracies can serve and build."

Governor Bricker has shown by example that state and local governments can be revitalized; that federal encroachment upon local affairs is not necessary for promotion of the general welfare; that in most instances a better job can be done by keeping government closer to home. In support of that stand he has had to fight attacks by federal bureaucracy and political smears from those who could not brook his opposition.

Bricker pledged his administration to "no increase in taxes," a promise so novel and startling that the *San Francisco Examiner,* in the midst of the excitement over the Golden Gate Exposition at its front door, celebrating the completion of the bridge across the bay, was impelled to remark editorially:

". . . if the state of Ohio, under the guidance of John W. Bricker, can make income equal expenditures, without new taxes, then Ohio will have contributed an exposition—an exposition of budget balancing—that will bring to the state greater credit and greater fame than could all the bridges and all the expositions combined."

The Governor's first words to department heads when he assumed office were that economy must be enforced, "no matter how distasteful." When the overloaded bureaus of the state government, on the Governor's orders, disgorged their unnecessary em-

7

ployees—more than 1,000 were dropped the first week of his administration, 500 from a single department—the *Pasadena Star-News* (California) declared that he was "doing the nation a real service by the example he is setting. What it would mean if the administration at Washington would follow Governor Bricker's example almost baffles the imagination."

Newspapers in Kansas and Georgia actively urged their states to follow the example of Ohio. In a Kansas Day speech at Topeka during the early days of his administration, Governor Bricker reminded his audience:

"When the American people in unmistakable language demand economy, economy will come. After all, we are entitled not alone to the kind of government we want, but the kind of government we are willing to work to get."

Many Ohioans kept their fingers crossed even after the Governor's prompt beginning on the economy program. Said the *Marietta Times* (Ohio): "Stern determination and strength of character will be required to make his policy permanent. When he has done so, he will have stood the most severe of tests."

Bricker has stood the test and maintained the course upon which he set the administration of the state's affairs. He took over a government with a $40,000,000 deficit, pared its operating budget, effected economies large and small, restored the state to a pay-as-you-go basis, met all obligations on time,

8

and soon was laying away something for a backlog. Today the state treasury has an unencumbered surplus of about $70,000,000 with which to face postwar economic conditions.

The aggregate of the state budget is larger today than when Bricker became governor, owing to larger subsidies for social security, public schools, and local governments, and to larger appropriations for the maintenance of the 23 welfare institutions of Ohio and her 6 state universities. The ordinary day-to-day operation of the state departments costs the taxpayer less in 1943 than in 1938, despite a recent 10 per cent increase in the pay of state employees.

To some extent the state's improved fiscal condition is the result of improved business conditions and the resulting larger yields from excise taxes; but to a very large degree it was brought about by improved and uniform administration of tax laws—the closing of loopholes, the stopping of leaks—and to unrelaxing enforcement of economies. The reductions in pay rolls and maintenance costs early in 1939 were no flash in the pan, but an indication of the Governor's permanent policy.

In midsummer of 1943 the state pay roll was $200,000 a month less than in October 1938, a reduction possible in spite of the 10 per cent pay increase to department workers, and in several cases to highway laborers, because the number of employees had been reduced 20 per cent. In the fall of 1943 there were 4,500 fewer in the three big departments—

highway, public welfare, and liquor control—than there were five years earlier.

Fiscal affairs have been so much improved throughout the state that local goverment debts are $100,000,000 less in 1943 than in 1938. Ohio ranks thirty-first among the states in per capita property tax, with $27.28, as compared with $61.48 in New Jersey at the top. It ranks twenty-fifth in all state and local taxes, the per capita amount being $58.83, as compared with $111.41 in New York. For every $100 in income received by Ohioans, $9.12½ goes into local and state taxes. In that respect Ohio is fortieth among all states. No state or local income taxes are levied in Ohio. The levy of most general application is a 3 per cent consumers' sales tax enacted in 1934.

As Bricker demonstrated his abilities and his record unrolled, his name figured more and more prominently in national political discussions. Early in 1939 the *Kansas City Star* declared that with Bricker's election the Republican party "could step forward with confidence ... could become not merely a party of protest and criticism, but a party of militant constructiveness." Almost at once Bricker was mentioned in widely separated parts of the country as a presidential possibility. Upon his re-election in 1940, his presidential chances rose, and they were substantially increased as he became a national spokesman against the continued centralization of government in Washington and the relentless expansion of federal bureaucracy. When he was elected to a third term in 1942, his candidacy was practically a foregone conclusion. Senator Taft announced that he would support Bricker for President in 1944 "if he decides to run." Taft declared: "In my opinion his administration of the government of Ohio has been notable among all the states in the Union."

Governor Bricker's attention was largely taken up with a session of the legislature until late in June 1943. Then he began to present to the people of the United States his views on foreign policy and other national issues. He began to emerge as an active candidate for President. Meanwhile, increasing pressure was brought to bear upon him to make an open avowal. On November 15 he came before the people of the United States as a candidate for President with the following statement:

"The Presidency of the United States is the most exalted office in the world. Grave problems will be presented during the term of the next President. Victory is now assured to the cause of righteousness in the war.

"Our Army, Navy, and Air Forces are fighting great battles and winning notable victories, and they will continue to final triumph under our proven military leaders. They have under their command the bravest, the strongest, and the best. As a result of our fighting, the United States will be in a position of great power and responsibility among the

11

nations of the world. All that power should be exercised with the deepest conviction that we have a great destiny to fulfill in America. We must keep ourselves strong, liberty-loving, self-governing, and use that power and influence throughout the world to bring about better international relations and to prevent the deadly destruction of war.

"We are a proud people. We need apologize to no nation on earth for our determination to preserve American liberty and individual opportunity against any odds, and we will defy any power that attempts to take from us any part of our heritage or weaken our position of leadership. Our purpose always should be to help others to lift their standards, but never to lower ours. There must be responsible participation by the United States in postwar co-operative organization among sovereign nations to prevent military aggression and to attain permanent peace with organized justice in a free world.

"The New Deal has come to the end of its service to the people of the United States. Confusion and distrust reign throughout the land. We need not alone a change of administration, but a change of the philosophy of government held by many New Dealers. The playing of one class of our people against another, the building of pressure groups by government, must come to an end. There is a need for impartial and just administration as between all classes, groups, and individuals in our society. The American people must be encouraged to look forward to the day as soon as possible after victory when government restraint will be relieved, rationing with all its implications will end, business will be encouraged, and individual liberty and opportunity restored. When sound government economy is established and our own nation made self-reliant, we can help other peoples of the world. Pledges should be carefully made and loyally kept. A candidate's word and a party's platform are solemn covenants with the people of the country. They must be kept to restore confidence in our government at home and faith in us among the nations of the world.

"In view of the great needs, confident of the fact that the Republican party will be called upon to lead our nation at the next election, I shall be a candidate for President of the United States in the Ohio primaries and before the Republican national convention."

CHAPTER II

CHILDHOOD

NOTHING IS MORE typically American than boyhood on a midwest farm at the turn of the century. Work was from sunup to sundown, mechanical aids to labor few. By the time a child started to school he had already learned the stern creed of hard work, frugality, and thrift. Each year he took on new duties in the round of chores the succeeding seasons bring. There was wood to cut, stables to clean, corn to hoe, hay to make, grain to thresh; there were horses to curry and harness, cows to milk, and pigs to feed. In the fall apples must be picked, wagonloads of orange pumpkins brought in from the field, corn cut and shocked and husked; and then the round began again.

But first, in the earliest and carefree years, the child sensed only the prodigal richness of fields, orchards, and barns—sunlight and wind on green and golden fields; the round firmness of apples, the scents of hay and fruit and flowers—the abundant rewards of hard work honestly done.

That was the background of John Bricker, born on one of the rich-soiled farms which checker the level expanse of Madison County, Ohio, a little southwest of the center of the state. In that country the fields are large and regular, neatly fenced; farmhouses shelter under groves of oaks and maples, which often slope off into the smaller, sparser growths of orchards. Some of the houses have grown out of log cabins, their rough sides now covered with clapboard or masonry to make them conform to the style of later structures. There are many small farms, but also some of the largest in the state. Large or small, however, none are show places; they are productive functioning farms, most of them worked by third- or fourth-generation owners.

In a log house on a small farm in Pleasant Township, six miles north of Mt. Sterling and twenty miles southwest of Columbus, John and Mary Ellen, twins, were born to Lemuel Spencer and Laura King Bricker on September 6, 1893.

Both the Brickers and the Kings had been farmers and pioneers for generations. The Reformed Church in Frederick, Maryland, lists John and Jacob Bricker (sometimes Brucker or Brucher) among the inhabitants of Frederick County in 1762. John, the Governor's great-great-great-grandfather, and his younger brother Jacob were born in Poltz, a small town in southern Germany, in 1725 and 1740. The great eighteenth-century migration from Switzerland, southern Germany, and the Netherlands to escape religious persecution brought the brothers to America, where they settled in Maryland.

15

By 1769 John Bricker had acquired three farms, totaling two hundred acres. He and Anamaria, his wife, had seven children, the oldest of whom was also named John. This second John served in the Revolutionary War as a corporal in Captain Philip Sawder's company of Colonel Ludwig Waltner's German regiment, Continental Line, recruited from Baltimore and Frederick counties. He and his wife, Nancy Boyd Bricker, had a family of seven girls and four boys. He started the family's migration to Ohio by moving westward in 1810 into Allegheny County, Maryland, where he settled on one of two farms he bought there. It was one of his sons, Jacob, who crossed the Ohio River to found the family in Madison County.

Jacob's son James Henry, the Governor's grandfather, and Lemuel Spencer, his father, were both born on farms in Madison County, as was his mother, Laura King. The Kings were of Scotch-Irish stock; and, like the Brickers, had come from Maryland.

When John Bricker was a boy, life revolved about three centers only: the home, the school, and the church. He had the good fortune to find in all three the same high standards of conduct and morality, the same reverence for lofty thinking and plain living.

The setting of his home changed three times, but the heart of it was his mother, who made of each house the same refuge and source of strength for her children. When John and Ella, as his sister was always called, were three years old, Lemuel Bricker

Ella and John Bricker at the Age of Three

McKendree School and the Twins' First
Schoolteacher, Mr. Charles Wilson

bought a 90-acre farm with a better house and moved his family there, where they stayed until the children were nine. He sold that farm and moved to a 100-acre one which had been Laura Bricker's home before her marriage. At the same time he bought a nearby farm with another 100 acres and worked the two together until his death. All three farms on which the children lived were in Pleasant Township.

One September morning when the twins were six, Laura Bricker handed them each a slate and a cardboard box of lunch, boosted them into a high-water buggy, and drove off with them to McKendree School two miles down the road. Forty-four years later Charles Wilson, the schoolmaster, remembers her that morning, sitting erect on the buggy seat, her large, strong hands grasping the reins firmly, her wide shoulders thrown back proudly as she answered his casual, "Well, Laura, you're starting them to school, are you?"

"Yes," she replied, "I want them to get an education so they can do the more good."

McKendree School, a red-brick building with large windows, a big stove, and a leaky roof, was the little red schoolhouse of American tradition, where pupils from six to seventeen studied and recited in one room, wrote on slates that screeched sometimes inadvertently and sometimes purposely, and sat at desks scarred by the jackknives of their fathers and older brothers. Blackboards were fastened to the wall; a row of hooks held the children's hats and coats; and their lunch boxes rested on a shelf above them.

The pasteboard box, so clean and shiny that first day, was expected to last out the year, and before many weeks had passed the row of boxes on the shelf grew so worn and battered it seemed they couldn't be made to do; but somehow they always did.

In the yard was a well with an iron pump and two outhouses at the back of the clearing. Recess time and noon hour were the times when the boys proved themselves in competition, wrestling, running races, playing "dare base" and "shinny." John's speed and co-ordination were quickly noticed, and he became one of the first to be called in games where sides were chosen.

Classroom work came easily to John because he could concentrate well. He was usually prepared when called on and easily found the words to express himself. He soon developed a fondness for history, and has been a keen student of it all his life.

For the three years they went to McKendree School, John and Ella walked the two miles there and two miles home again, usually across fields, picking up a crowd of children as they went, playing tag to lengthen the distance as often as not. Their mother took them to school in the buggy only if the weather was stormy. The move the family made when they were nine meant a change to Toops School, which required them to walk only a quarter-mile each way.

Their amusements were simple ones, and usually

games played without toys. They valued their few possessions because they earned or made them for themselves. John made a sled for himself and Ella, but he could not make a slate, so it was a proud day in his life when he possessed a double slate, such as the elite at school had, instead of the poor "single" with which he started.

One of the biggest events of the year was their summer trip to Magnetic Springs, Ohio, where Uncle Bill King ran a hotel. The trip lasted only three or four days, but John always found a place on the baseball team.

His first experience of pride in wages received for labor done came to John at nine years old, when he "hired out" to his father to pull milkweed out of the cornfield for fifty cents a week. When he was a little older, his father gave him permission to leave the farm on holidays if he hired a substitute to pitch hay or plow corn, or whatever he had to do. John seized the chance to play baseball, not only because he loved the game, but because he discovered that he could earn more catching for a team than it cost him to hire a substitute for farm labor.

There was seldom a time when there wasn't work to be done, but occasionally Lemuel Bricker and his son would slip off to the sycamore-shaded banks of Deer Creek to fish in quiet companionship. There was good fishing in the creek, which ran in front of the farm a half-mile away. Bass, bluegills, sunfish, catfish, and rock bass rose to their homemade lines.

Then, too, there was the "Bobby Hole," where six to a dozen boys of the neighborhood would plunge in on a summer's evening to cool their sweating bodies.

Going home through the moonlight, the scent of new-mown hay heavy on the air, was a good time to make plans for the future. At first John's thoughts went no farther than high school in Mt. Sterling, but gradually he began to think forward to college and the life afterwards. Sometimes John King, his cousin, would join him and his father in their fishing expeditions or go hunting with them in the surrounding fields and woods. John King was a dozen years older than John Bricker, and the boy looked up to him with all the admiration a boy of ten can feel for a young man. As he heard the future jurist talk about his plans to study law, John Bricker began to think he, too, wanted to be a lawyer.

In Ohio at that time pupils in country schools had to pass a special examination before they could enter a high school; an examination called the Boxwell, after the legislator who sponsored the law which made it compulsory. As a rule the Boxwell was taken at the end of the pupil's eighth year. Bricker passed it at the end of his seventh, but went another year to Toops School before striking out for high school.

John and Ella went regularly to Sunday School at nearby rural churches. The Governor remembers that they were completely interdenominational in their earliest association with the church. They went for a time to a Methodist Sunday School, then to a United Brethren church, and finally to the Christian Church at the crossroads of Antioch. The last was the church at which he first took communion and joined the church, and there he was superintendent of the Sunday School when he was sixteen.

CHAPTER III

YOUTH AND EDUCATION

THE MONTH they were fourteen, John and Ella Bricker started to high school. The sun was barely up when they hitched Molly, the family mare, to their buggy and drove off to Mt. Sterling, their new salmon-colored pasteboard lunchbox on the seat between them, and new adventure before them.

In the village John arranged to stable his horse in a barn just over the fence from the two-storied, slate-roofed red brick school building. The first morning he noticed three or four other boys stabling their horses, too, bigger and older boys. At fourteen John had not yet started to get his growth, and on that chilly September morning in 1907 he felt small and green and "countrified."

He was a quiet boy, and for the first few months he attracted little attention. He did his work and re-cited well but not brilliantly. His early interest in history grew, and he read and reread everything on United States history he could find. For the rest, he felt his way slowly.

Every school day for the next four years, the Bricker buggy, drawn sometimes by a sorrel and sometimes by a bay, stirred up the dust or churned the mud of the six miles between farm and village. There was one exception—a morning when the road was too slick with ice for their unshod horse, and John walked the distance in an hour and a quarter rather than spoil his attendance record. He did not miss a day of high school in the whole four years.

Through most of the school year, the sun would come up when they were halfway to town, and in winter it was always dark by the time they reached home. After that, John still had six or seven cows to milk before he was through for the day.

The drive to school was generally a lively affair. Brice Connell, a neighbor boy who became superintendent of schools in nearby Derby, rode with them regularly, and one day he and John fell into an argument. As the dispute grew more heated, the boys jumped out of the buggy to settle the matter with fists. Scarcely had they squared off to do battle when Ella shrewdly whipped up the horse and set off down the road. The boys forgot their dispute and dashed after the buggy, yelling to Ella to wait. When she thought they had been properly worn down, she brought the mare to a stop and let the chastened boys climb in.

At noon recess time, John and Ella would climb into their buggy in the stable and open up their lunchbox, the envy of the town pupils who went home for luncheon. Yeast biscuits left over from breakfast and made into pork sandwiches were packed into the box along with apples, thick wedges of pie or whatever else was in the farm pantry that morning. These were the lunches upon which the Johns and Ellas from the farms of the Middle West throve in those days before school cafeterias.

John made his place in school life through two interests which have bulked large throughout his life: debating and sports. He made the debating team, and impromptu ball games in the school yard led to a place on the baseball team. It began to be noticed that John invariably became the leader in any group. He played on one of the best ball teams Mt. Sterling high school ever had, the one which beat Columbus North High by 15 to 2, and won other games in Columbus.

Baseball has been a major passion with Bricker since boyhood. He organized a team of his own in the neighborhood and kept a diamond mowed in his father's pasture. Frank Toops, now manager of the New York office of Travelers Insurance, headed the rival team they usually played. Until the time he entered college he earned money playing on various teams, but he gave it up then to preserve his amateur standing. Today the Governor follows the fortunes of the Cincinnati Reds as avidly as any other fan. He has helped to open the major-league season for them, showing something of his old-time form. He has been known to halt an official journey, leap out of the car, and run across the street for a newspaper, explaining, "I want to see what the Cincinnati Reds did today."

As John grew taller and gained in confidence, he began to notice the girls and they him. He had a good horse and buggy, which was equivalent to having a roadster with the top down nowadays. Socially, John was a success.

The Bricker house was always a center for the young people of the neighborhood. After John and Ella went to high school, they brought week-end guests to share in the diversions of farm life, from hauling pumpkins to horseback riding and baseball. In winter it might be bobsledding, usually in connection with "Big Meetings," a series of religious revivals. The sled would drive through the neighborhood, picking up the young people to take them to whichever of the crossroads churches was holding the meetings.

Several of the boys who were John's guests then and later in college, became lifelong friends, among them Freddie Patz, now a lawyer in Lincoln, Nebraska, and Barton Griffith, an attorney in Columbus.

John learned to dance and began going to parties, usually with his sister. The night of the Junior-Senior banquet, when they were Juniors, was the night when the earth passed through the tail of Halley's comet, and there was much excited speculation as to whether the human race would be gassed out of existence. The youngsters at the dance, however, saw an incident so startling as to take their minds off the comet—John Bricker slipping away for a buggy ride with someone else's girl. When they came back, noticeably later, a wit remarked in the ensuing turmoil, "I guess they thought if they were going to be killed by Halley's comet, they might as well die happy."

The commencement exercises of the class of 1911, when John and Ella graduated from high school, were held in the Christian Church, and each member of the class delivered an oration. As a matter of course, John chose a political subject, "Direct Election of United States Senators." An amendment to the Constitution had been proposed to elect senators by popular vote.

Being a student of history, John knew the reasons which had prevailed in the Constitutional Convention of 1787 for selecting the upper house by the less direct but more deliberate method of election by state legislatures; and because the reasons seemed to him good, he spoke against the amendment.

The townspeople had come to know John well in the four years of his high school course. "Fine-looking young one, and got good sense, too," they said. In his turn, John had a deep affection for the town, an attitude which has never changed. While in college he took the presidency of the Mt. Sterling high school alumni association, and asked Edward Snyder, a Mt. Sterling furniture dealer, to be chairman of the membership committee. Snyder said he was too busy.

Ella and John, with Their Parents, at the Time
of Their Graduation from High School

The Governor and His Sister (Mrs. P. Freeman Mooney)
Today

"If you want a job done, get a busy man to do it," John replied.

Snyder finally agreed to take it—if John would give him a Washington job when he became President. They have laughed about it often since then.

John had decided to be a lawyer, which meant going to law school at Ohio State University in Columbus. The cash return on a farm is never very large, and he had to earn some money himself before he could get started. At the same time he wanted to live at home to help on the farm, and teaching a local school seemed the only answer. Accordingly, the seventeen-year-old boy called on the school board the spring he received his high school diploma. One of the members whose son would be starting to school in the fall remarked that he would be satisfied to have John Bricker be the boy's teacher. The board agreed with him, and the following September saw John once more in a red-brick schoolhouse, this time a teacher in the Robinson School, two and a half miles from home.

His salary was $45 a month, and to that he added an extra $5 for acting as janitor of the building. More interested in the years ahead of him than in teaching itself, John nevertheless was a satisfactory teacher in the eyes of the parents and school board. His pupils ranged through all eight grades, and one of them at least was older than he. Perhaps because he was six feet tall and broad in proportion, weighing 170 pounds, with some local fame as an athlete, he had no trouble maintaining discipline. One boy learned from his teacher to pitch a curve ball which made him a local baseball star.

When school closed early the next May, John had saved $450, and his father told him to go ahead to college next fall because he could give him some help.

In September 1912 he packed his trunk and set off for the college of arts, philosophy, and science at Ohio State University. He took a room near the campus in the home of friends—relatives of his relatives—and usually went home week ends.

As in high school, Bricker found himself slowly in college. Ohio State was a big university, thirty times or more the size of his high school; and the social graces he had learned in the village could not armor him against feeling gauche in comparison with the young sophisticates who lolled on porches of big-pillared fraternity houses, spoke a puzzling jargon of their own, wore dazzling and inscrutable pins, often set with jewels, and sported the latest in men's wear.

The fact that Ohio State is partly an agricultural school helped John to feel at ease and learn his way about. Imperceptibly he got ahead, and before long was a leader not only among boys from farms, but on the campus as a whole.

In his Sophomore year he was catcher on the varsity baseball team. By the end of his Junior year, he was secretary of the university Y.M.C.A., a debater well above average on the varsity debating team, and president of his class—with a good scholastic record besides. That year he was initiated into Delta Chi and moved into the fraternity house.

In the spring he was one of the dozen men "linked" by Sphinx, the honorary society of seniors. "Linking" was the highest accolade a Junior could receive, for it meant that he had made a name for himself on the campus and was particularly chosen by the outgoing class to carry on the campus traditions. The ceremony always took place at noon on a spring day before a crowd comprising almost the entire student body, gathered in front of old "U" hall.

In his Senior year in arts college, Bricker was elected president of the university Y.M.C.A., and at Christmas and Easter recesses he went on tour with a "Y" team which held meetings in several Ohio towns, telling high school students the fields of activity open to them at Ohio State and describing life at the university, with primary emphasis on religion and service. Among Bricker's teammates on these trips were several of the university's outstanding athletes, including Charles W ("Chic") Harley who, the next fall, would be chosen an all-America halfback by Walter Camp.

Debating was a major campus and intercollegiate activity in those days. Sometimes a hundred students would try out for the varsity teams, the number gradually being narrowed by competition to provide an affirmative team and a negative team of three members each, and an alternate for each team. Bricker made the varsity team in his Junior year in arts and his Junior year in law. In the intervening year, he did not try out.

Professor V. A. Ketcham, chairman of the Speech Department at Ohio State, recalls that Bricker showed marked ability to analyze public questions. "John was an outstanding debater because of the careful, systematic way in which he looked into questions, because of his thoroughness and accuracy in finding the facts, because of the soundness of his reasoning processes, and because of the accuracy of his conclusions."

Against Indiana University, at Bloomington, in his first year as a varsity debater, Bricker took the negative side on the question: "Resolved, that the federal government should own and operate the telephone and telegraph systems of the United States." The negative side won by unanimous decision of the judges.

Two years later, Bricker was captain of the affirmative team which debated Cornell on the question: "Resolved, that the United States should adopt compulsory military training." The First World War was about to engulf America and the debate caused a good deal of excitement on the campus, particularly when the university's first debating victory over an eastern college was achieved under Bricker's captaincy.

John Bricker was never more startled than when the physical examination given him at the time of his matriculation at Ohio State revealed that he had an abnormally slow heartbeat. He had never been sick, except for the diseases of childhood, and he had always been as active as the next fellow. But the university doctors discovered that his heart beat only 55 times a minute, as compared with the normal 72, and they barred him from taking the gymnasium classes required of all Freshmen and forbade him to participate in track, football, or basketball.

Boylike, Bricker felt ashamed of his slow heart, but he did not let it discourage him. Nothing had been said about not participating in baseball, a major sport at Ohio State, so he decided to try out for the varsity nine. He signed up as a candidate for first base and was trying out for that position when Director of Athletics L. W. St. John, who was then also the university baseball coach, called him over to the bench and asked him if he ever had caught. Bricker said yes. It was the truth because he had caught one game in high school.

The way Bricker tells it now, there was a serious dearth of catcher material for the team, the job devolving almost solely upon one good catcher, and St. John decided to give him a try. In the chain of ensuing circumstances, Bricker thinks he got a break better than he deserved.

In an early game with Ohio Wesleyan, Bricker showed up well behind the bat. The *Ohio State*

Lantern, the university paper, reported that "Bricker led the assault, gathering a single and a double in four times at bat." He also made six put outs and one assist and committed no errors.

Midway in the more strenuous part of the season, the first-string catcher, Louis Pickrel, caught the mumps and was on the shelf for most of the remainder of the schedule. Bricker, the Sophomore, caught seven and one-half games that year, including some of those against the big Western Conference opponents, and made a creditable showing. He wasn't a heavy hitter, but his fielding record was nearly perfect, and the coach liked him for his enthusiasm and perseverance.

A frequent battery for Ohio State in that spring of 1914 was Trautman and Bricker, the pitcher being George M. Trautman, now president of the American Association. Jack McCallister, scout for the Boston Braves, likes to tell a story about that battery. He says that several times during the 1914 season, he was directed to scout Bricker and that on each occasion he found it impossible to observe Bricker's catching ability due to the fact that Trautman always happened to be pitching, and he could never get the ball past the batter. In the years since then, the Bricker-Trautman battery has been reunited on numerous occasions for special ceremonies at the Red Bird Stadium, home of the Columbus team in the American Association.

A game that stands out in Bricker's memory was

the one played that same year against the University of Chicago at Chicago. It was Bricker's first game in Western Conference competition and, incidentally, his first visit to a really big city. The pitcher for Chicago was Des Jardens, who stood six feet six in his stocking feet and pitched a fast ball that looked to Bricker like a B.B. shot thrown out of one of the tall buildings he had seen that morning. Rolly Cook, now a lieutenant colonel in the U. S. Army, pitched for the Buckeyes and threw a spitter that day that not only baffled the Chicago hitters, but gave Bricker a strenuous afternoon behind the plate. For the rooky catcher, there was a perfect ending, however, for Ohio State won 6 to 1.

The next year, with the regular catcher's return, Bricker's backstop duties were curtailed, but he still did sufficiently well to deserve election as president of "Varsity O," the organization of athletes of all sports who have won their varsity letter.

The Governor has always felt at home with athletes. One of his best friends is Billy Southworth, manager of the St. Louis Cardinals, who lives near Columbus. When he met Jack Dempsey at a public event in which they both took part, he was pleased with their visit together; and he enjoyed talking to Harry Kipke, former University of Michigan athlete and football coach when he visited Columbus on Navy Recruiting Day. He is a football as well as baseball fan, and has known personally nearly every Ohio State player in the past thirty years. He frequently visits the team in their dressing room after a game, a privilege his varsity letter affords him; and until recent wartime restrictions on travel, he followed the team on most of its out-of-town trips.

All the time of his college course, John kept his roots on the home farm. The summer between his Sophomore and Junior years, he and Ella ran the farm while their mother and father went on a trip to Maine, the only vacation he remembers his parents taking. That was when his father gave up any lingering hopes that his son would make a farmer.

John drove his parents to Columbus in the family's recently acquired automobile, put them on the train, and started back to Mt. Sterling. On the way he stopped at the State Farm at Orient, where he found bull calves being given away. He signed up for four of them and later took them home to the farm. The Brickers had six cows, and milking them every night interfered with John's plans for seeing his girl every evening. His deep-laid plot was to let the calves milk for him, and before long he had only two to milk. He should have done one and Ella the other, but he made a dicker by which Ella milked both and he was free for his date.

Bricker received his bachelor of arts degree from Ohio State in June 1916. He had never "flunked" a course and had received several "merits," the highest grade given by the university. He "merited" in mathematics, foreign language, and some of his English courses; but the record still shows a condition in gymnasium—the course he couldn't take because the doctors said no.

Dr. W. O. Thompson, president of Ohio State, had been so impressed by Bricker's ability in debating and his general attainments that he offered him a new instructorship which was being established in the university's English department. He had also an offer of the mathematics position on the faculty of the Chillicothe High School, and was approached on the proposition of going to China to teach in a university. If it had been for only one year instead of three, he would have accepted. But he had his mind on the law and respectfully declined the proffered jobs.

Then, two weeks after John had received his arts diploma, Lemuel Bricker died. Ella had married recently. The family was breaking up. What would his mother do? John suggested that he stay at home and run the two farms, but Laura Bricker would have none of that. She knew her son's ambition to be a lawyer, and she felt that he should be. She answered that she had arranged it all—they would sell what they didn't need, she would move into town and direct the operation of the farms herself. She spent the last twenty-five years of her life in Mt. Sterling, but she remained to the end a farm woman. She continued to manage the two farms until her death, when she was seventy-eight.

The relationship between mother and son was

very close, however undemonstrative on the surface. When he was re-elected attorney general she sent him a plain white card bearing the simple words, "Dear John: Congratulations. Mother." His mother was the first to hear from the candidate himself the results of every election until the time of her death.

The fall after his father's death, Bricker returned to Ohio State to complete his education in law. As he did not want his mother to be too alone in the early months of her widowhood, he commuted to college from Mt. Sterling. During that school year, from September to June, five days a week, he would catch the B. & O. train every morning at 5 o'clock, curl up on a narrow plush seat or stretch his long legs from one seat to another if the coach wasn't too crowded, and finish out his sleep as the train rattled twenty-five miles to the capital in the dimness of dawn. Every evening, around five, he would board the return train in Columbus and study on the way home, arriving shortly after 6 o'clock. It was a tiring schedule, even for a strapping young man of twenty-three, but he missed only one day of college that whole year.

Professor George W. Rightmire, later president of the university and now president emeritus, who had Bricker in his law classes, recalls him as an "earnest, sincere, industrious, alert, and responsive" student. "He always was able to convert the abstruse rules of the law into everyday rules of conduct." Dr. Rightmire asserts. "He showed then, as later when he was a member of the Public Utilities Commission and attorney general of Ohio, an ability to make the law solve the facts and give an intelligible answer. As I look back upon his law-study days, I feel that they were characterized by the guiding principle that law must be alive and effective in society—a social force— or it is nothing."

Bricker's circle of friends at the university widened continually. Serious-minded in the main, he nevertheless was popular, and his hearty laugh generally could be heard above those of the others in this or that little group knotted on the campus between classes or at one of the High Street sandwich and soda shops.

He was handsome, too, one of the tallest men on the campus, broad-shouldered, straight as a ramrod. His hair was jet black, parted on the left, the rest a slightly wavy shock combed to the right. His taste in clothes was conservative, but his collars, in the accepted college style of the day, were high and choking, his ties of heavy silk, knotted big as a butternut.

Through his many activities, he began to be elected to so many posts of honor and importance that he gained the reputation of being a campus politician. His Delta Chi brothers razzed him with the nickname of "governor," but there was a note of admiration in their tone.

CHAPTER IV

WORLD WAR I

IN APRIL 1917, John Bricker was in the midst of preparations to take the bar examination; but when the United States declared war on Germany, he immediately went down to the recruiting depot hastily set up on the campus and applied for enrollment in the first officers' training camp at Fort Benjamin Harrison.

Everything went well in the preliminaries, until he reached the physical examination. The doctors listened to his heart, bent closer and listened again, then waved him aside. His heart was too slow—men with heartbeats three-fourths the normal rate were not being accepted.

The sharp disappointment he suffered that day dogged Bricker through twenty months of war, and even now is not wholly forgotten. He went back to the campus bitterly frustrated to begin an unavailing struggle to get into action. He tried to enlist in the Army as a private; he tried the Marines and the Navy. None of them would have him—it was always the same story: "Everything fine except that heart."

In June he registered in the draft and took the

state bar examination, which he passed despite having another year at the university before his course would be completed. Then a call to report to his draft board gave new life to hope. Maybe the draft authorities weren't as strict as the officers' training, the Army, the Navy, the Marine Corps had been.

But this time, too, he heard the familiar words: "Slow heart—rejected."

Bricker had his share of stubbornness. He had never been stopped in his life, and he didn't intend to begin now. He enlisted for war work with the Y.M.C.A. and was assigned as athletic director to the 329th Infantry, 82nd Division, at Camp Sherman. Many Ohio boys whom he knew were at the camp in Chillicothe, and he came to know hundreds more. He coached them in baseball and directed other sports. One day a boy of foreign extraction called him "Johnny de Brick," and the regiment seized on the appropriate nickname. Thenceforth he was "Johnny de Brick" to the 329th.

Bricker liked his work and the men liked him. He might have been happy if it were not for his consuming fear that he would be left behind when the day came for the regiment to entrain, bound for France. One day he spoke of his dread to Lieutenant Colonel John Toffey of the 329th—father of the Lieutenant Colonel John Toffey who led American boys in the capture of Sicily in 1943.

Colonel Toffey admired Bricker's determination and listened sympathetically. He had a suggestion to make: The regiment was entitled to two chaplains, and only one post was filled—and that by a man who knew nothing about sports, recreation, or entertainment, but gave his energies to strictly religious activities. Why didn't John apply for the other chaplaincy? Then he could go wherever the regiment went and take charge of recreation, entertainment, and morale.

Colonel Toffey sent Bricker off armed with a letter to Colonel James W. Furlow of the Quartermaster Corps:

Camp Sherman, Ohio
May 26, 1918

Col. James W. Furlow,
Quartermaster Corps,
Washington, D. C.

Dear Dad:

This will introduce to you Mr. John Bricker who has been associated with our local or Regimental Y.M.C.A. since the organization of our Regiment.

He is a splendid man wherever you put him. A college graduate, excellent athlete and has tried every known method to get in the Army, but has been turned down on account of an athletic heart.

I advised him to go to Washington and if someone could only put him right, that is, tell him where to go and who to see, I believe he might be able to get what he wants.

He now wants to get an appointment as Chaplain, and I do not hesitate in the least to state he would make an ideal one.

If you can give him a start or tell him who to see or where to file his application etc., it will be greatly appreciated by me as I really believe him worthy of some consideration.

Sincerely yours,

JOHN TOFFEY, JR.
Lt. Col. 329 Inf.

Life took on a new face for Bricker. He filed his application at once with the adjutant general and followed it up with a trip to Washington to speed up the official decision before the 329th got its sailing orders. In Washington he was told that the appointment would be approved—provided he was an ordained minister.

Weary and disheartened, John went home to Mt. Sterling to spend a week end with his mother. On Sunday he and his mother went to church service in the little Christian Church to which they both belonged. After service the pastor, Rev. C. C. Ryan, shook hands with John, and of course asked how he was getting along. On impulse, Bricker told him all about his troubles.

"John, I believe maybe I can help you," said Rev. Ryan. "Let's see what I can do."

A special meeting of the Central Ohio Christian Conference was called to meet at Lee's Creek in Highland County. The conference decided to ordain John Bricker as a minister of the church for one year for the specific purpose of permitting him to serve as a chaplain in the Army. He was not to preach, however, they stipulated. That authority was reserved for men who had attended divinity school.

41

So, in his own church in Mt. Sterling, on the evening of Thursday, February 28, 1918, John Bricker was ordained a minister (for one year) in the Christian Church. In its account of the ordination the Mt. Sterling paper commented, "He is the type of young man any community would be proud to claim."

The race against time continued. Now that he was ordained, he applied again for a chaplain's commission. Before taking up his new work, he would have to take a training course for chaplains, lasting about six weeks. There were already signs and rumors that the 329th was moving out. The days passed and no word came from Washington.

Finally the regiment received the orders which moved it to the coast for embarkation. Hoping that there might somehow still be time for his commission to come through so he could sail with the regiment, Bricker boarded the train with the 329th and accompanied it to Camp Merritt, New Jersey. A few weeks later "Johnny de Brick" stood on shore and watched the regiment board ship and sail for France.

Thoroughly disgusted, he went back to Camp Sherman, and there his authorization came through and he was assigned to Camp Zachary Taylor for the chaplains' training course.

Lieutenant Colonel Toffey had requested that Bricker be assigned to the 329th upon his commissioning and sent to France to join his old outfit. Bricker hoped against hope; when he completed the course in the late spring and was commissioned a

Graduation from Arts College,
Ohio State University, June, 1916

U. S. Army Chaplain,
World War I

first lieutenant in the Chaplain Corps, his assignment was to Camp Eustis, Virginia, a coast artillery center.

Within a few weeks of his arrival, Camp Eustis was hard hit by the influenza epidemic which swept the military camps. "Men are dying like flies," the camp authorities reported. The commanding officer sent for Lieutenant Bricker and told him he was being assigned to the hospital to do what he could. The camp was short of help and Bricker unattached.

A mask tied across his nose and mouth, Lieutenant Bricker walked into the hospital which was to be his field of labor for three heartbreaking, nerve-wracking months. There were 300 sick men when Bricker began, and for several weeks the number grew. John Bricker had never seen anyone die; now he saw men die who had become his friends—men who talked and laughed with him, who told him about their girls and their families; men who talked big and fearlessly, men who had been shy.

They were dying and they knew they were dying. Sometimes they sent for him in the middle of the night. They gave him messages to take to "Mom" and "the girl." Sometimes he wrote letters for them. Sometimes they were just scared because the man on the next cot had died.

Bricker read to them, or perhaps they only wanted to talk. It seemed to him that they talked perhaps more freely to him because he wasn't actually a minister and they felt no embarrassment with him. Sometimes they frankly asked for the Bible. He helped men of all denominations, finding their places for them in a prayer book or *Science and Health*, as the case might be.

A motorcycle and sidecar was assigned to Bricker, with a rider. Jolting over rocky roads, through endless days of drenching rain or burning sun, through moonlit nights, he rode in the sidecar running down things the men craved and could not get in camp. He raced over the countryside hunting drugs, candy, tobacco, books—whatever the men wanted most. Sometimes he was too late when he got back, but many times he returned to a warmer "thanks, fellow!" than he has heard anywhere else in the world.

He helped arrange the bodies of men for burial, helped put them in their coffins, went to the train to see them off home to the little burial grounds he could picture in his mind—like the ones in Madison County, Ohio. He sorted the belongings of the dead men, sent things home, wrote letters. For a long time after the war was over, Bricker was still carrying messages to mothers and fathers in small towns and cities of the Middle West.

Through it all he was never sick a day. He never took medicine, although once in a while a doctor or nurse would look at his hollow eyes and drooping shoulders and give him a stimulant, and he would go back to work, ready for more hours of strain.

It was an experience which Bricker never talked about much in after years; it was too close to him.

When the flu epidemic had died down, Bricker

decided to try again for line service. About the first of November his application was approved with the qualification that he would have to accept a demotion to second lieutenant and take six weeks of training at the artillery school at Old Point Comfort. Bricker was willing to accept the demotion and prepared to take the training when the Armistice came. Six weeks later, he was mustered out of the service as a first lieutenant of the Chaplain Corps.

One incident in Bricker's fruitless trip east with the 329th became a turning point in his life. En route from Camp Sherman to Camp Merritt, the troop train stopped briefly at Columbus. Although none of the soldiers were allowed to leave the train, Bricker, in his Y.M.C.A. uniform, swung to the platform which had become so familiar to him in the months when he was commuting daily from Mt. Sterling to Columbus to his law classes, intending to pick up some newspapers and magazines.

On the platform he ran into a group of girls and recognized among them his cousin, Arema O'Brien, assistant dean of women at the university. The cousins kissed affectionately, which focused the attention of all the girls on the tanned, black-haired soldier. Hasty introductions followed, and Bricker thought slim, brown-eyed Harriet Day was the prettiest girl he had ever seen. When he went back to the troop train he carried in the back of his mind a picture of her warm, smiling face, her grace and charm.

And Harriet Day remembered Arema's good-looking cousin.

As soon as he was discharged from the Army, Bricker returned to Ohio State University to finish his interrupted course in law, despite the fact that he had already passed the bar examination and was entitled to practice. In the winter months of the beginning of 1919, he settled down to studying and took up again some of his old activities.

One spring week end the campus Y.M.C.A. and Y.W.C.A. scheduled a joint conference at Groveport Inn, a few miles southeast of Columbus. On the interurban Bricker sat next to Harriet Day, president of the Y.W.C.A., and he discovered at once that she was even prettier and more charming than he had remembered. The trip was very short, but not short enough to keep Harriet and John from finding out that they had many mutual tastes. In the few days of the conference they spent a good deal of time together, always finding more to talk and laugh about. The day after the conference Bricker asked for a date; at a dance in town that week he asked to visit her family the following week end. John had heard that he had serious competition, and he was taking no chances—it was a whirlwind courtship. Mr. and Mrs. Rudolph Day approved of the young man their daughter brought home with her, and Harriet felt that she had known him always. Within three weeks of the streetcar ride to Groveport, she had promised to marry him.

46

The next winter, while John was finishing his law course, Harriet taught chemistry, general science, and history at the high school in Urbana, her home town. John spent week ends at his mother's in Mt. Sterling that year and learned to drive the crooked road from Mt. Sterling to Urbana with his eyes closed. On September 4, 1920, two days before his twenty-seventh birthday, John Bricker and Harriet Day were married.

CHAPTER V

THE GOVERNOR AT HOME

BRICKER HAD FOUND a promising opening in the law firm of Postlewaite and Martin, whose offices look down upon Capitol Square—the squat, solid bulk of the gray stone statehouse, the sweep of grass plaza before it, and the dull bronze figure of McKinley gazing at the hotel across the street from the spot where he stopped each morning on his way to the statehouse and turned to wave to Mrs. McKinley seated at her window.

From a small stucco-pillared house of brown shingle in the suburban village of Grandview across the street from the Community Church, John commuted to his office in downtown Columbus, beginning a steady, unspectacular rise to prominence; while his young wife did the housework and learned to create the atmosphere of a home.

On a beginning lawyer's earnings, it was a simple, frugal home, typical of thousands to be found in any section of the country. On Sundays the young couple walked across to the services in the Community Church, an interdenominational church, then in the experimental stage, made up of members from nearly thirty denominations. Harriet had been brought up an Episcopalian, and John still belonged to the Christian Church (now the Congregational-Christian); but they both joined the Community Church in Grandview and have been active in its affairs ever since. At various times, Bricker has served it as trustee, deacon, and chairman of trustees.

Both the young Brickers were family people, and Sunday was likely to bring Harriet's mother or John's to spend the day. Or else the young people traveled down to Mt. Sterling, where Mrs. Bricker, Sr., could fill up her big son with fried chicken, mashed potatoes, and lima beans—or perhaps pigs' knuckles and sauerkraut. "Those are the things he likes best," she used to say. "John never was much for salads."

In the first years of their marriage, John would run down to Mt. Sterling and borrow his mother's car when he wanted to take a short trip. The Brickers have never been great travelers. A few times to Florida, Washington, New York, annual Governors' Conferences in various places is about the extent of their travels together. Bricker himself has covered practically every section of the United States on business trips, but neither of them has been to Europe. "John probably never could afford to go to Europe," explains a friend; "and the Brickers don't do things they can't afford."

A daughter born to the Brickers early in their marriage died in infancy, and shortly afterwards they

49

adopted a baby boy, Jack Bricker, now thirteen years old.

Jack has the kind of father every boy dreams of— one who likes hunting, fishing, riding, baseball, and carnivals—and does all of them well. Father and son go fishing together just as Lemuel Bricker and his son used to; and the Governor's fishing companions declare that the father is harder to tear away from the trout stream than the boy. He is forever wanting to try the next riffle. A friend who has seen him in action with a fly rod says enviously:

"John can hold up his end with anybody in the world with a fly rod. He certainly can make it sing! I've seen him go out in a stream and in half an hour catch enough fish for the whole crowd."

Father and son share early-morning horseback rides, too; and not long ago the Governor appeared at his press conference in the statehouse with a welt across his face where he failed to dodge a low-hanging branch across the trail.

Time off for duck hunting has been a part of Bricker's program religiously observed even during recent busy years. Every fall when the season opened he packed up his gun to keep a standing date in the marshes of Lake Erie with friends—Howard L. Bevis, president of Ohio State University; L. W. St. John, director of athletics there; George Trautman of the Trautman-Bricker battery, now president of the American Association; James Lincoln, Cleveland industrialist and member of the university board of

50

trustees; and John Galbreath, president of the National Association of Real Estate Boards and a close personal friend from boyhood. The Governor's Airedale, Brownie, is in the Army now; but he prizes highly a golden retriever, Duke, recently acquired.

Bricker prefers a single-barreled shotgun for ducks and pheasants on two counts: first, it is light to carry; and, second, he considers that if he can't get a bird on the first shot, the bird has won the right to live.

The Governor takes the pleasure of a boy in county fairs. After he has seen the exhibits of livestock, 4-H Club, and Future Farmers, he and Jack yield to the lure of the midway and go off to pitch the ball for prizes, try their luck at shooting galleries, and eat cotton candy and ice cream. A better-than-average shot, the Governor can't resist a shooting gallery, and usually an audience collects to watch him knock down two targets with one shot. Once when he was shooting in a clay-pigeon trap at Castalia, only one man in the party could beat him, and that was Walter Hagen. But Bricker evened matters when he won a box of golf balls Hagen put up as a prize for the longest drive. Bricker plays golf perhaps half a dozen times a year, and his best score is 96.

The governor's mansion on East Broad Street has taken on many characters according to the temperaments of the different governors, characters ranging

51

from part-time office to an elaborate backdrop for parties. With the Brickers in residence, it is first of all a home. An easy and homelike atmosphere in a 27-room house, with the entertaining demanded of a governor's wife, is high tribute to Mrs. Bricker's skill as hostess and homemaker. She manages it herself without a secretary or housekeeper, catering for innumerable teas, planning and budgeting occasional large dinners—once she had a hundred dinner guests.

Mrs. Bricker once said to a home-economics group, a little wistfully, that she wished she had taken a course in tearoom management because she can never tell how many guests will turn up at a reception. But if any crisis has occurred in her kitchen, her quiet, dignified social skill has concealed any inkling of it. Beneath her gentle manner lies a spartan quality which the demands of entertaining occasionally call out. One day when she had sprained her ankle, she stood in a receiving line for two hours, wearing a bedroom slipper on her aching foot.

Keeping the mansion a normal home for her family is Mrs. Bricker's chief concern. The Governor raids the icebox at midnight like any householder. Jack and his friends have the run of the house, and hoarse shouts come drifting in from a game of football on the lawn or a game of catch with his father. Like his mother, Jack plays the piano, and music forms a strong bond of companionship between mother and son. At thirteen, of course, hunting and trapping and fishing are closer to the boy's heart, however.

His parents leave it to Jack what official functions he wants to attend, and occasionally he is curious to see what they are like. Some years ago he made his presence felt at a reception for the Republican national committeewomen by releasing two white mice from under his jacket.

Mrs. Bricker has not let public life interfere with family or friendship ties. Her mother, Mrs. Maude Day, one of the capital's most distinguished women, is her frequent companion; and until her death in February 1942, the Governor's mother was a regular visitor at the mansion. If she wasn't with him in Columbus for the week end and he could not get to Mt. Sterling to call on her on Sunday, the Governor never failed to talk with her on the telephone. His sister, too, now Mrs. Freeman Mooney, is a frequent visitor at the mansion with her husband and their daughter Laurabelle. She and Bricker own jointly the two farms which their father bought long ago. Mrs. Mooney manages them now and often drops in at the Governor's office on farm business.

Friends look to the mansion as a source of thoughtful kindnesses. Some time ago when Joseph A. Parks, dean of men at the university and a college friend, was ill in the hospital, it was Mrs. Bricker who thought to ask his small daughter to stay with her so that Mrs. Parks could spend her time at the hospital.

Charitable work has always taken a goodly share

53

of Mrs. Bricker's time. She is not content with lending her name, but goes to meetings, accepts chairmanships—in short, works. She is active in behalf of the Y.W.C.A., the Children's Hospital, and the National Society for the Control of Cancer. Since the war began, she has been chairman of the Nurses' Aide Committee of the Franklin County Red Cross, and one of the strongest forces behind its accomplishments. She speaks well and forthrightly, but seldom at political meetings. "That is John's sphere," she explains.

What time Mrs. Bricker can salvage for herself, she spends on music, painting, drawing—she makes no claim to artistry in any of them—or to tracing down a piece of antique glassware. Her collection of Baltimore Pear is particularly good, and often exhibited in hobby and antique shows all over the state. In the matter of collecting glassware, she is a real hobbyist, preferring to hunt down the items in out-of-the-way places. She refused her husband's offer of a dozen of her favorite Pear goblets for their crystal wedding anniversary, explaining that half the fun of owning them is the search for them.

Her intellectual hobbies are chemurgy, the science of finding new uses for products of the soil, and the advancement of medicine. As a girl she wanted to be a doctor; but when she was in college, teaching was almost the only "accepted" profession for a young woman, and she yielded to the persuasions of her family. Chemistry was the nearest she

MRS. JOHN W. BRICKER

could get to medicine, and at the university she is still remembered in the Department of Chemistry for the excellence of her work and her aptitude for research.

Columbus is Mrs. Bricker's native city—she was born within a few blocks of the governor's mansion —and her fellow townsmen take a proprietary pride in her dark-eyed charm, her social poise, her smartly turned out appearance. A newspaperwoman who came to Columbus to look her over in 1939 wrote of her grace of manner, "It would be as natural in the White House as in the most remote corner of the country."

CHAPTER VI

FLEDGLING POLITICIAN

POLITICS IS indigenous to John Bricker's life, rooted deep in his earliest memories. Lemuel Bricker went regularly to all the Republican meetings held in the township house of Mt. Sterling; and with him went his small son, still in grammar school. There, as the Republicans of Pleasant Township threshed out political issues and selected their delegates to county conventions, young John heard his first political debates, the first shouts of "aye" and "no" as he watched representative government functioning in its smallest unit.

In this atmosphere the boy absorbed the feeling that an active part in government is a natural privilege and responsibility—as natural as belonging to a family, going to school or church, earning a living. Long before he could formulate an abstract idea, he had an intimate impression of co-operative action, of decision and common purpose revealed through discussion, of the collective wisdom of all the people helping to fix the course of the nation—perhaps the most distinctive contribution America has made to social organization.

This interest in the active practice of government first found expression in Bricker's life in 1916, the year he cast his first vote for President. That was the year when Charles E. Hughes, former governor of New York and justice of the United States Supreme Court, was Republican nominee for President; and Frank B. Willis, later a United States senator from Ohio, was seeking a second term as governor. Bricker, then a student at Ohio State University, organized a Hughes-Willis Club on the campus, with the help of Paul M. Herbert, who later became lieutenant governor during the three terms of Bricker's governorship.

It was only natural that John Bricker should soon become an active worker in the Republican organizations of his home city. Almost immediately after leaving law school, he joined with John M. Vorys, later congressman from the Columbus district, to form a Roosevelt Republican Club—named, of course, for Theodore Roosevelt. At first the regular party organizations regarded the upstart club as a "young insurrection," but not long after, the new club was invited to merge with the traditional old-guard Buckeye Republican Club. One of the stipulations in the merger agreement was that one of the young Roosevelt Republicans should soon be elected to office in the amalgamated organization.

At about this time young Lawyer Bricker addressed a noon meeting of the Buckeyes and made a very favorable impression. The two circumstances combined to make him president of the Buckeye Republicans shortly after the merger.

In 1920, the year of his marriage and starting in law practice, John Bricker was offered a job in the Department of Justice in Washington; but he had already decided that his career in public service should start at home, and he could not be tempted out of Ohio. In the fall of the same year his first opportunity to hold public office opened up.

One morning as he rode downtown from Grandview in a streetcar, a member of the Grandview village council took the seat next to him, and in the course of conversation offered him the village solicitorship, an office he held for the next eight years. The duties of the village solicitor were light, but for Bricker it was important because it gave him his first foothold in the work for which he was so obviously fitted. "I have never known anyone except Bricker whose friends have thought, from the time he was eighteen years old, that he would some day be governor and even President," says Hugh K. Huntington, treasurer of the Republican state organization in Ohio.

In the years from 1919 to 1923, John Bricker's energies were largely devoted to building up his practice and promoting the interests of Postlewaite and Martin. In the meantime his professional and personal horizons widened as he quietly took an increasingly large part in the life of his city. Businessmen in Columbus discovered that the serious-looking young lawyer, mild-mannered, low-voiced, was excellent company. They liked his direct glance, his companionable conversation, his interested attention when they talked. He had the essential of popularity, a real and lively interest in people.

Because he has always enjoyed the fellowship of other men and believed in co-operative effort by the group, Bricker joined clubs and organizations of various kinds—the Odd Fellows, the Eagles, the Moose, the Masons. For several years he was president of the Central Ohio Area Council of the Boy Scouts, covering nine counties. Today he is an active member of the Supreme Council of the Ancient, Accepted Scottish Rite, Thirty-third Degree Mason, and his work in the Masonic orders gives him great personal satisfaction. He is a trustee of Denison University, Defiance College, and Franklin University.

An organization in a lighter vein was the Cole Slaw Club, a group of university friends, lawyers, and real-estate men with whom Bricker frequently lunched at an unpretentious restaurant. When Bricker was first elected governor, the Cole Slaw Club presented him with his first silk hat to wear at the inauguration ceremonies—and then at the last moment Bricker refused to wear it.

An appointment as assistant attorney general and counsel for the Public Utilities Commission came in 1923 and gave Bricker the preparation for the work on the commission which established him in the public eye as a champion of economy and fair prices

59

to the consumer. It was no happy accident, but his own thoughtful choice which gave Bricker that particular assignment in the attorney general's office.

The Republican candidate for attorney general in 1922 was C. C. Crabbe, a native of Madison County who had taught the Toops School just before the Bricker twins were registered there. John Bricker worked hard on Crabbe's behalf during the campaign; and when he was elected, Attorney General Crabbe offered him an appointment to the attorney general's office. Only one job there would interest him, Bricker replied; counsel for the Public Utilities Commission. Crabbe was keeping an experienced man in that post, so the job was not open then; but in October of 1923 the Attorney General called Bricker on the telephone one day and offered him the post, with the title of assistant attorney general.

The state was just beginning its program to have the Utilities Commission regulate commercial motor transportation, and the usual number of test cases of a new law came up. Bricker tried case after case in courthouses all over Ohio, before the Ohio Supreme Court, federal district court, and even the United States Supreme Court and the Interstate Commerce Commission in Washington. He argued over 150 cases before the Ohio Supreme Court alone, members of which told Attorney General Crabbe that no one prepared his cases as well as the young assistant. When Bricker left the office upon change of attorneys general in 1927, he had a knowledge of public utilities law second to few in Ohio.

Back in private practice—the firm was now Postlewaite and Bricker—John Bricker found himself restless for public life. He had liked the busy tempo of the attorney general's office—the pressure for time and action, the consultation and preparation of cases, the argument and rebuttal before courts and commissions. Competition with wily, experienced counsel had stimulated him far more than college debating—and besides, he was doing something for the progress of society and government.

In 1928, when he was thirty-four, he ran for the Republican nomination for attorney general. The signers of his declaration of candidacy numbered three judges of the state supreme court, a judge of the federal district court, a common pleas judge, the president emeritus of Ohio State University, the mayor of Columbus, the city law director, the president of the Columbus Bar Association, and the state commander of the American Legion.

There were six men in the race this first time that John Bricker ran for a public office. He campaigned energetically, and his speeches show that already he had discerned a cloud on the horizon of government. He was warning even then against "allowing the dead hand of paternalism to thwart our development." With the whole state for his stumping ground, he missed only one scheduled campaign meeting—and that because his car rolled off the gravel road within sight of Steubenville, his goal. By the time he got a tow car and had the car back on the road, the meeting was over.

When the votes were counted in the primary, Bricker had carried 60 of the 88 counties, but came out second in total vote, 8,797 behind the winner, which was approximately one vote per precinct short.

The four years until Bricker's second try for the attorney general's office were largely filled with his service on the Public Utilities Commission. In November 1929 Governor Myers Y. Cooper appointed him to the commission to fill out an unexpired term. It was a fortunate time for Bricker, in that the nature and far-reaching consequences of the cases which came before the commission during his term brought his abilities to the attention of a wide audience. Cases which involved tremendous corporation values and fixed rates for large sections of the state had been pending for years, and a large number of them finally came before the commission in the years between 1929 and 1933.

In the Ohio Bell Telephone Case, Bricker set the tentative valuation figure which was the basis of the rate later established. It took several years to fight out all the issues in the courts and effect a settlement; but in the end the rates were reduced and telephone subscribers in Ohio received a refund of $7,225,000 for excessive rates paid in the past.

The Cambridge Telephone Company case was the means of delivering a blow to certain utilities holding companies throughout the country. The Cambridge Company was a subsidiary of a holding company domiciled in another state, which controlled and interlocked with other companies in several parts of the country. The holding company customarily charged the various subsidiaries for administrative expenses; and the commission found that, instead of being an advantage to the subsidiaries, by sharing among them the expenses of administration, this custom meant that the holding company was being paid over and over again in full for its rather doubtful administrative services. By refusing to allow these charges in computing the rates to be charged against telephone subscribers, the commission struck a mortal wound to utilities holding companies five years before they were outlawed by Congress.

The extension of electricity in rural areas was another achievement of the Public Utilities Commission. No new administrative agency was set up, no public funds spent; the commission merely issued an order in 1930 requiring electric light and power companies to extend their lines into rural areas when petitioned. The commission stipulated that the rates charged the farmers should be simply a percentage return on the companies' investments; and there should be no heavy initial connection charges or similar assessments over a long period of time which would have the effect of higher, and sometimes prohibitive, rates. As a result of the extension order, Ohio led all states in rural electrification several years before the Rural Electrification Administration was established by the federal government. And today Ohio leads all states in the number of farms using electricity.

John Bricker had been named to the commission as a recess appointment, which meant that his name would have to be submitted to the Ohio Senate at its first sitting for confirmation. The Senate which sat next was a new one, brought in on the rising Democratic tide of 1930—the same tide which defeated Governor Cooper's bid for re-election. Cooper was still governor when the new Senate met, however; and he submitted Bricker's nomination to that body, composed of 18 Republicans and 14 Democrats. The Democrats immediately argued that the new Democratic governor should choose a utilities commissioner in order to put his party in control of the important Public Utilities Commission during his administration. With 17 votes required, the Republicans had enough to confirm Bricker against the opposition of the Democrats; but 5 Republican senators balked; and Senate action was delayed for several days.

A meeting between Bricker and the 5 senators was arranged. Knowing that the trouble was factional within the Republican party, since no charges had been made against him or any reasons stated during the deliberations, Bricker took the senators at a disadvantage by asking them outright to give their reasons for opposing him. The senators said they thought the valuation he had set in the telephone case was too high; it would hurt the party. Bricker replied that he had arrived at the valuation figure by careful, painstaking judgment—that he considered it a fair value. He had no inclination to urge them to one course of action or the other, said Bricker; they could do as they pleased. But if they wanted honesty in the handling of utilities rate cases, that was what they would get if he were confirmed.

The senators liked his answer and the insurrection petered out. One senator returned to the floor of the Senate to make a speech urging confirmation of Bricker, and the Senate consented to the appointment by a vote of 17 to 6, one Republican being absent for sickness and 8 Democrats either absent or sitting silent.

Bricker was an advocate of speedy settlement of cases. He was instrumental in clearing many long-pending cases from the commission's docket, and he opposed long recesses and continuances in cases affecting the rates paid by the public. When there was an inexcusable delay in determining the Columbus gas rate in 1932, his resignation forced a decision in a case which otherwise might have been delayed for months—perhaps beyond his term as commissioner.

The Columbus gas-rate case had state-wide importance because it involved several procedural precedents which would result in lower consumers' rates if established. After long, careful trial, the case was taken under advisement. Bricker did the part of the work assigned to him, wrote his opinion on it, and settled down to wait for the conference with the other commissioners which would decide the final rate. Month dragged after month and Bricker could not get a conference arranged, until he came to the conclusion that his colleagues were not trying to reach a decision. He immediately submitted his resignation to the Governor.

At this time Bricker was Republican nominee for attorney general, and Governor White thought he saw a chance to embarrass him by refusing the resignation and ordering Bricker back to his job. Bricker replied that he would go back to his desk only if the Governor instructed the commission chairman, his appointee, to get busy. The resulting publicity brought a speedy decision of the case.

Under a city ordinance, Columbus consumers were paying 48 cents per 1,000 cubic feet for gas. The gas company was asking the Public Utilities Commission to establish a rate of 65 cents. In a minority opinion, Bricker held that the 48-cent rate was "reasonable, just, and lawful, and sufficient to yield a reasonable compensation for the service." The other two members, one a Republican, the other a Democrat, signed a majority opinion fixing the rate at 55 cents. Both the city and the gas company appealed to the Ohio Supreme Court, which upheld Bricker's minority opinion on every point in which it differed from the majority one, and ordered the commission to fix the rate at 48 cents.

The company then appealed the 48-cent rate order to the United States Supreme Court, which reversed the Ohio court on one point. The Ohio Supreme Court, upon being remanded the case, then ruled that the rate should be somewhere between 48 and 55 cents. Meanwhile, the five years covered by the ordinance had expired; and the court pointed out that, since the consumers had paid the 48-cent rate part of the time and the 55-cent one the rest of it, the average rate had been about 50 cents for the period, which it ruled to have been fair and just.

Thus Bricker's 48-cent opinion had the effect of holding down rates in Columbus, even though it did not prevail in all particulars. But the case had a significance far beyond the gas-rate in Columbus: it slowed the general rise of utilities rates, even before the Bell Telephone case, of similar import, had ultimately been disposed of; and it set new rate-making precedents.

The Columbus case was the first in which the Ohio Public Utilities Commission tried to determine the actual cost of natural gas, from the producing wells to the burner tips in the consumers' homes. It went into the valuation of the properties of various affiliated companies, instead of accepting on their face certain charges made by one affiliate or subsidiary of a big corporation to another. It fixed not only a rate at the gate of the city to which the gas had been brought from the well, but a rate at the state line where gas came across the Ohio River from West Virginia to mix with the Ohio gas. These rates were of great importance in fixing subsequent rates in other Ohio cities, and consumers were saved millions of dollars.

Bricker had been a member of the Public Utilities Commission not many months when utilities consumers and subscribers of Ohio realized that in him they had a champion. They felt that with John Bricker on the commission, they were getting a fair deal in the rates fixed. Not that Bricker adopted the role of crusader against the utilities companies; he merely went at his job objectively and fought for principles and cold figures alike, and his reasoning and his figures were almost invariably upheld in the courts of review. His three years on the commission are a milestone in the long struggle to establish rates fair to consumer and corporation alike.

Meanwhile, Bricker was growing steadily in the estimation of Republican party leaders, as well as the average citizen. In 1930 the campaign managers chose him to be party spokesman in a debate with the Democratic candidate for the United States Senate before the Cleveland League of Women Voters, and similar important speaking assignments fell to him in the ensuing months.

In the spring of 1932, Bricker announced that he

would be a candidate for the Republican nomination for attorney general. He had the distinction of having no primary opponent and was elected the following November. Franklin D. Roosevelt carried the state by 74,376; the Democratic governor was reelected by a plurality of 204,585; a Democratic lieutenant governor, secretary of state, and chief justice of the supreme court were elected; only 6 Republicans were sent to Congress out of the state's 24; the legislature went strongly Democratic; courthouses were turned over wholesale to the Democrats —but Republican Bricker was elected attorney general by a plurality of 10,008.

CHAPTER VII

ATTORNEY GENERAL

ATTORNEY GENERAL BRICKER took office in January 1933, a time calculated to try out quickly the quality of his political and social thinking. Depression-created emergencies in unemployment relief, the conservation and liquidation of banks and building-and-loan societies, and financial distress of local governments demanded his attention, in addition to the usual duties of his office—formidable enough in normal times.

Much of the substance of the public law of Ohio is written in the opinions of the attorney general. Although he is not a policy-making official, he frequently determines the direction or extent of an administrative policy, and sometimes even of social and economic progress, through his interpretation of the law as enacted by the legislature and decided by the courts. He may be overruled by the courts, or the legislature may override him with subsequent enactments; but, failing this, his opinions are the law, and he is as a rule upheld by the courts and respected by the legislature.

Through his gigantic law office passes all the legal

business of the state. He is counsel for all the state departments, giving them legal advice and representing them in courts ranging from justice of the peace to the Supreme Court of the United States. In the course of the year the various state officers, departments, boards, bureaus, and commissions, as well as the prosecuting attorneys of the 88 counties, raise some 1,500 or more diverse questions of law to which the attorney general must render formal opinions. In addition, he and his staff are almost constantly in consultation with these various agencies over their legal problems, and he prosecutes all claims of the state for moneys due it.

During Bricker's four years, his office rendered 6,645 formal opinions and tried 3,913 cases in the courts. He collected $6,170,054 in delinquent claims, a million dollars more than had been collected in the four years just preceding. At the same time he operated the department for $35,441 less than the cost of the preceding four years and turned back to the state treasury at the end of his term $45,000 of the funds the legislature had appropriated for his second term.

Immediately after the Bank Holiday of March 1933, Attorney General Bricker had to assume responsibility for all legal services to the liquidators and conservators of 263 state banks—178 of which were liquidated and 85 operated on a restricted basis. Similar responsibilities devolved upon him in the liquidation, sale, merger, reorganization, and rehabilitation of building-and-loan associations throughout the state.

Bricker's term as attorney general substantially established the present body of law in Ohio relating to the liquidation of insolvent financial institutions. The official opinions he gave, the cases tried, the counsel given by his agents were largely responsible for Ohio's leading the nation in the liquidation of banks closed during the depression, returning to the depositors an average of 84 per cent of the deposits of completely liquidated banks.

So carefully and wisely did Bricker select the counsel that not one defaulted out of 250 attorneys employed. Moreover, the liquidation costs to depositors were low. The attorneys' fees allowed were about half, in some cases only a third, of the amounts allowed in other states in comparable instances, and a good deal less than the fees allowed in national bank liquidations in the same localities—justifying once more the Founding Fathers who held that experiments and activities of state governments should point the way for the federal government.

One of Bricker's ablest and most far-sighted opinions was on the subjects of old-age pensions and unemployment insurance. On April 3, 1933, he upheld the constitutionality of proposed legislation before a committee of the Ohio legislature, some two and a half years before President Roosevelt signed the New Deal's social security bill. Seven months after Bricker's opinion, the voters of Ohio declared

72

for old-age pensions, and Ohio was paying them months before Congress passed the Social Security Act.

Bricker's opinion on unemployment insurance plainly pointed the way a progressive government could travel toward broader social and economic concepts. In a workmen's-compensation case many years earlier Mr. Justice Pitney had ruled:

"A machine as well as a bullet may produce a wound, and the disabling effect may be the same."

Attorney General Bricker qualified it to read:

"An *idle* machine as well as a bullet may produce a wound, and the disabling effect may be the same."

Ten years later it would be the accepted policy of the nation that unemployment is as crippling as war and as much an obligation of the government. But all Bricker could do was to say that the proposed law in Ohio would be constitutional in every respect; it remained for the legislature to decide whether it wanted unemployment insurance as a state policy. Not the Democratic body Bricker advised, nor its Democratic successor, nor the influence of two Democratic governors produced an unemployment-insurance law until 1936.

During these years when a large part of the public looked to Washington for the answer to all problems, Bricker was warning against "federal encroachment" in state, local, and private affairs. As attorney general he was vigilant for Ohio's rights and successfully defended her laws in several cases before the United States Supreme Court.

Minimum wage-and-hour laws for women and children was a fiercely controversial subject. The Supreme Court had ruled that New York's law was unconstitutional. In face of this decision Bricker contended for Ohio's law before a three-judge federal district court and won his case. The Supreme Court later reversed its decision. Through Bricker's efforts the courts also sustained an Ohio law prohibiting the employment of women on specified dust-creating machinery.

Ohio's right to prohibit the importation of goods made by prison labor was successfully defended by her attorney general. He also established the right of itinerant workers, or their dependents in case of death, to receive workmen's compensation for industrial injuries suffered while employed in Ohio, whether the employer was domiciled there or in another state. In a New York case before the Supreme Court he filed an intervening brief arguing that a state has a right under its police power to regulate the sale and distribution of milk and fix minimum milk prices. The law involved in the case was upheld by the court, a decision which supported the Ohio Milk Commission.

As attorney general, Bricker was as watchful of the rights and welfare of individuals as he was of state rights. He upheld the legality of contracts for hospital service to individuals, under which persons of low and middle incomes could insure themselves adequate care in case of sickness. In 1934 he held that the Ohio Civil Service Commission did not have the power to require an applicant for a civil-service examination to state his race or submit his photograph. He ruled that a person charged with a crime or a material witness cannot be held incommunicado by any public official.

The state supreme court upheld the Attorney General when he argued for the constitutionality of laws granting war veterans who pass civil-service examinations a 20 per cent raise in their grades, and gave preference to veterans over nonservice men with equal grades. He also won a decision from the supreme court that county officials could not circumvent civil-service laws by the subterfuge of appointing their employees as deputies.

A deep reverence for the meaning of the American flag led Bricker to rule that a board of education is within its rights in compelling students to salute the flag and take the oath of allegiance. A statement made later during his governorship clarifies his motives in this stand:

"There is no religious connotation in saluting the American flag. Loyalty to the flag and to the government that it represents strengthens and never weakens one's religious convictions. The flag is a guarantee of your right, as well as that of every other citizen, to his religious belief."

That was his answer to an appeal from a religious

75

sect which forbade saluting the flag. The courts had refused to compel the director of agriculture to rent them a state building, and they appealed to the Governor.

Another of Bricker's opinions bearing on the influence of public schools was a ruling that they must not subject their pupils to sectarian influence. Religion has always held a firm place in Bricker's own life. He has attended church and been active in religious circles in a modest way; but religion with him is not a creed, it is a way of life.

Representing the Public Utilities Commission, Bricker continued his efforts to save money for the consumers. In eight municipalities served by the Dayton Power and Light Company, $350,000 was returned to the consumers when the state supreme court decided in favor of Bricker. The United States Supreme Court also upheld the commission, requiring the West Ohio Gas Company to refund about $250,000. In still another Utilities Commission case, Bricker won a decision from a three-judge federal district court, saving large sums to coal consumers in the Youngstown area.

Holders of insurance policies made substantial savings through the Attorney General's successful defense of the state Division of Insurance in several important cases. The state supreme court also upheld the Insurance Division in refusing to license a company because of misleading advertising and other practices contrary to the laws protecting the policy-buying public.

When federal and state prohibition were repealed, Ohio pioneered in establishing a state liquor monopoly. Bricker upheld the constitutionality of the law, winning three cases before the state supreme court, and one before a special three-judge federal district court. He ruled that a warehouse whisky receipt was a security under the "blue sky" law of the state, and their sale or transfer was subject to the regulations of that law. Better Business Bureaus made wide use of this opinion against persons who sold the receipts at scalper's prices to people who knew nothing about distilling and had no idea what they were really buying.

Two instances in which the state legislature refused to accept the Attorney General's opinion were in cases involving the legislature itself. Bricker ruled that it was unconstitutional for the legislature to extend the terms of incumbent elective county officials. When the legislature persisted, and the Governor tried to sign into law a bill extending the terms of incumbent county recorders, Bricker took the case to the state supreme court and won it. The same court sustained him in his ruling that members of the legislature could not vote themselves allowances for board and lodging or other expenses in addition to their salaries. To a man so scrupulous that he has never turned in an expense account for traveling expenses in all the time he has been in public office—who has never even been paid for making a speech—this was anathema.

As early as 1934, pressure was brought to induce Bricker to seek the Republican nomination for governor. He had hardly begun his term as attorney general when the state supreme court upheld the 48-cent gas rate for Columbus which he had recommended the year before. Already it was widely recognized that his minority stand on the Public Utilities Commission had checked the upward flight of Utilities rates and would be directly responsible for lower gas rates in several cities. Almost overnight he was boomed for governor, but his characteristic patience and conservativeness, his desire to establish a solid record of public service, counseled him to wait at least another two years. After another term as attorney general, he felt, he would be ready for the governorship.

His popularity and public respect for his judgment increased steadily. The public took note that his opinions and arguments in court were both sound and progressive—that they pointed always toward giving Ohio good and responsive government.

The Democratic sweep in 1934, when Bricker sought re-election, brought in Martin L. Davey as governor and sent a second Democrat to the United States Senate. It was an uphill fight for any Republican, and Bricker had to leave on official business for Washington before he learned the results of the election. Every newspaper he saw on the way carried headlines to the effect, "New Deal Sweeps Everything." Bricker argued a case before the Supreme Court and returned an imperturbable "I don't have the least idea" to questions about his success. It was only after he returned to Ohio that he learned that he had commanded a majority four times the size of his margin in 1932.

During his second term, Bricker was in a position to witness, at close hand, the administration of Governor Martin L. Davey which through Senate investigations and court litigations became famed for charges of "shakedowns," "kick-ins," graft, and corruption. It was characteristic of Governor Davey to seek to excuse a specific charge on the ground that the act complained of was either "legal" or that "it always has been done and will continue to be done long after you and I are dead."

When accusations were made against the Governor himself, he answered charges with countercharges, filing libel and slander suits against his accusers and quietly withdrawing them after public interest died down. Once he went so far as to press charges through a preliminary hearing, but the court refused to bind the defendant over to the grand jury. He even filed a slander suit against Harry L. Hopkins, then WPA administrator, daring him to come to Ohio and get himself arrested. When Hopkins had a speech scheduled in Ohio, Davey obligingly withdrew his suit.

It was commonly accepted among business concerns that, in order to do business with the State, it was necessary to "kick in," sometimes at regular intervals, with contributions to Democratic state headquarters where the Davey-chosen chairman held sway. To Attorney General John Bricker, the prevailing method of operating the state government was, at once, abhorrent and a clear challenge. In 1936, he determined to seek the Republican nomination for governor and oppose Davey for re-election.

He was nominated without opposition and plunged into a vigorous campaign in which he charged the Davey administration with collusion and corruption. Repeatedly he told the voters that a "slush fund of a million dollars" had been raised by shake-downs and kick-ins to re-elect Davey.

The Governor, for the most part, ignored the charges and did not even threaten to file the usual libel and slander suits. He relied upon two things to re-elect him: his smoothly functioning state machine and the New Deal, then at the crest of its power. He had been at odds with President Roosevelt all through his administration and had vehemently assailed certain phases of the New Deal; but he correctly divined the best breeze in which to fly his kite in 1936.

At that time the presidential and state tickets were printed on one ballot in Ohio. Davey took "straight-ticket voting" as his campaign slogan, so there would be "no chance of Roosevelt being defeated," he told voters, because splitting the ticket might make their votes invalid.

Nearly half a million voters did split their tickets in the election, but the President's landslide was so irresistible that it swept the fractious Governor back into office. Roosevelt carried Ohio by 619,285 votes; Davey by only 126,688. Bricker, on the contrary, ran far ahead of his ticket—300,000 votes in front of the presidential nominee.

Sharper to Bricker than the sting of personal defeat was his disappointment that the electorate had failed to repudiate the type of government which he felt Davey represented. He could take courage, however, from the fact that no Republican candidate for governor could have stood up against that Democratic victory, the heaviest in Ohio since the birth of the Republican party. Only two Republicans were sent to Congress in a delegation of twenty-four; every Democratic candidate on the state partisan ballot was elected; and the most overwhelmingly Democratic state legislature in eighty years was chosen.

CHAPTER VIII

CAMPAIGNER

GOVERNOR BRICKER can look back and say, "I have always walked away from a good law practice to accept a public office. I have always come back to a better practice than I had before." When he returned to private life in 1936, he resumed his practice with conspicuous success in the old battle against rising utilities rates. In 1937 and 1938 he served as special counsel for the cities of Columbus, Toledo, Akron, and Norwalk in gas-rate litigation.

His practice was by no means confined to utilities cases, however. In March 1938 he was trying a case in common pleas court in which his client was asking damages for the death of her husband in an automobile collision with a truck operated by a large manufacturing company. He had rejected the company's last-minute offer of a compromise settlement, for something like $10,000, so that he felt great responsibility for the outcome of the case.

His concluding statement to the jury fell on the morning of the day he had planned to issue a statement on his candidacy for governor. He delivered a brilliant argument, then left the courthouse to meet the press, leaving it to associate counsel to let him know the verdict. A telephone call in the midst of his conference with the capital newsmen informed him that the jury had awarded his client $30,000.

In the years between 1936 and 1938, the public learned more about the Davey administration. It came out that the state's contract for trucking liquor had been let to a company which owned not a single truck. The dummy concern got the contract for 17 cents a case and sublet it to a bona fide trucking outfit at 11½ cents. Eventually the contract was outlawed by the courts, and during Bricker's administration the state recovered $113,740 from the bogus company.

During the legislative season of 1937-1938 a special committee of the preponderantly Democratic state Senate produced testimony substantiating the charges Bricker had made against the Davey administration during the campaign. In a formal report the committee described the condition of the state government as "unbelievable." It had found "padded expense accounts, falsified reports, forged bills, pretended statistics, even punishment of those politically opposed, rake-offs and commissions and pay-offs."

In the Department of Liquor Control the committee found "the entire situation so shot through with forgery, corruption, graft, false reports, faked statistics and maladministration, as to be hopeless of cure." In the Highway Department it saw "the sad spectacle of almost gleeful waste of taxpayers'

83

money." The Purchasing Department was "so plainly run in defiance of law as to cause this committee to be bewildered. . . . It is not to be wondered at that the state's money has been doled out to political favorites at just twice what should have been paid by the taxpayers."

In an effort to work out some kind of reply, Governor Davey arranged for an independent investigation of the Highway Department by a board of inquiry composed of professors of engineering. Unhappily, the board backfired on him by reporting that the state had purchased bituminous concrete at "excessive prices"; that some contracts had been let "under conditions indicating manipulation of awards by the department"; and that "a number of contracts" had been let "without complying with legal provisions."

Grand juries in several counties, one under Attorney General Herbert S. Duffy, a Democrat, began looking into charges of wholesale shake-downs of civil-service employees for campaign contributions. Indictments were returned in three counties. In the capital, where several prominent administration figures had been indicted, it proved impossible to get convictions; but in another county the state highway director, Ivan Ault, was convicted of soliciting contributions from a civil-service worker. He was fined $300 and sentenced to 30 days in jail, but Davey pardoned him immediately. The civil-service law, said the Governor, was a "dead letter."

In face of these revelations, the people turned to the man who had reported these irregularities to them in 1936 with so little effect. By March 1938 Republican committees in 48 counties had formally adopted resolutions urging Bricker to run again.

Governor Davey announced that he would seek re-election, but the Democracts undertook a "purge" and rejected his third-term bid. They nominated Charles Sawyer, their national committeeman, as their candidate.

Bricker campaigned under the slogan, "Ohio needs a change"; but he also offered a positive program to the voters—a reduction in the cost of state government, payment of the school deficit of over $17,000,-000; improvement in the administration of relief and old-age pensions; putting all government costs, including the financing of public schools and poor relief, on a pay-as-you-go basis; a balanced budget; enactment of strong antigraft legislation; and "honest government efficiently administered by incorruptible state officials."

"I consider the paramount issue to be honesty, efficiency, and common decency in the conduct of the state's business," he told listeners in tents, fair grounds, schoolhouses, churches, grange halls, public squares, and street corners throughout the state.

Inexhaustible energy and a catholic interest in people made campaigning more stimulating than arduous for Bricker. It was not unusual for him to drive 1,500 miles a week, sometimes alone, doing his own driving, sometimes with a caravan of cars filled with members of the campaign parties. In either case a paper sack full of apples went with him, and as he rode he munched apples or occasionally smoked a cigar. When he had someone to drive him, he made use of his time on the road to read letters and campaign documents. In later campaigns he could sleep while he rode late at night by thrusting his head into the "doughnut," a special contraption devised by a friend. The "doughnut," named by the campaign members, is a large padded frame which fits around Bricker's head and supports it against the swaying of the car.

A lively interest in the ways and thoughts of country people is a heritage from Bricker's boyhood. As he drove through the country between rallies he sampled the road stands to replenish his apple bag and dropped into small-town lunch counters for a glass of milk and a piece of pie—coconut cream if possible, and if there was only one piece left, he and his party flipped for it.

To this day one of the Governor's favorite reminiscences is of an encounter in a little general store in one of the hilly counties down by the Ohio River. He found a lunch counter there and stopped for the usual piece of pie. As he was leaving, his eye fell on a glass case, and in it something he used to see in the crossroads stores of Madison County when he was a boy—ranks of "Star" and other brands of chewing tobacco.

Governor Bricker and His Son Jack
at a County Fair

Casting with Fly Rod in an Ohio Stream

"Good heavens!" he ejaculated. "I haven't seen J-T plug in forty years! That's the kind my dad used to chew. I didn't know they made it any more!"

"Yep," replied a bystander. "They's a danged lot o' spittin' in them plugs."

Bricker tried to plan his campaign tours so that he could get back to Columbus every night and spend some time in his office each day. Sometimes he covered a whole congressional district, anywhere from three to nine counties in extent, making from fifteen to twenty speeches a day. Even with this schedule, his voice was as clear on the last speech as on the first.

His experience in court, added to his long interest in debating, had made Bricker a skillful and compelling speaker. Especially when he spoke extemporaneously, piling one telling point on another, his fists swinging in emphasis, his hair rumpled by his intensity, his eyes alight with conviction, he brought his listeners up cheering.

After the speech he liked to slip into the crowd and ask pointed personal questions of individuals about how the campaign was going; and he always remembered exactly how close to or how wide of the mark his informants came.

The CIO figured prominently in the campaign in that year of sit-down strikes. It opposed Davey in the Democratic primaries because of his calling in state troops in the "Little Steel" strike in 1937; but when Sawyer won the nomination from Davey, the

CIO supported him. The Ohio State Federation of Labor, affiliate of the AFL, issued a report to the effect that Bricker's record was favorable; but the CIO and Labor's Non-Partisan League, its political offshoot, attacked him viciously. In stating his position to organized labor, Bricker said:

"I have always been a friend of organized labor. . . . I believe that labor has the right to bargain collectively. I believe that labor has the right to choose its own representatives for bargaining purposes. I believe that labor has the right to strike and the right to peaceful picketing. Government should protect labor in the lawful exercise of these rights.

"I do not believe that labor has the right to take possession of an employer's property under any circumstances. Sit-down strikes are illegal and must not be tolerated. They will not be tolerated by me when I am governor. I do not believe that any labor union has the right to compel any worker to join against his will. . . .

"As governor, I will be governor of all the people. I will not permit a dispute between management and labor to result in terrorism or in the collapse of civil authority. . . . Neither gangsters nor labor racketeers will dictate to me when I am governor of Ohio."

The 1938 election swept in the entire Republican state ticket, with Bricker leading in number of votes. He lost CIO strongholds in Cleveland, Akron, Youngstown, and a few other industrial centers; but he carried 77 out of the 88 counties and had a majority of 118,225. Robert A. Taft became the first Republican national senator from Ohio in ten years. Fifteen Republican congressmen were elected as against nine Democrats, reversing the trend of the past eight years. The state legislature went as overwhelmingly Republican as its predecessor had been lopsidedly Democratic.

The Governor-elect met with the Republican members of the legislature a few days after election to map out plans for the change in government he had promised, and began to choose his cabinet.

At two o'clock in the afternoon, 25,000 people stood on the lawn of the statehouse facing the Doric columns of the west portal. It was January 9, 1939; and John William Bricker was about to take the oath which would make him the fiftieth citizen to become governor of Ohio. The occasion was a turning point in Ohio's history. She was weary of bungling in state affairs, distressed at the treasury deficit and obligations unmet. She had repudiated the old ways and turned to a man who had promised her "sanity in public affairs, stability in public policy, honesty in public conduct, integrity in public office."

His tall bulk accentuated by formal morning dress, John Bricker stood bareheaded on the platform in front of the crowd, waiting for the ceremonies to begin. Behind him his wife, his seventy-five-year-old mother, and his sister Ella formed a smiling background. Bands played, confetti drifted down from the buildings across from the capitol, a man in the crowd frantically waved a clean new broom. James Garfield Stewart, mayor of Cincinnati, waved a greeting from the back of an elephant, one of a herd which had been marched onto the plaza. Eight-year-old Jack sat astride the platform railing, his eyes glued to the cannon where national guardsmen were preparing to fire the salute to the new governor.

Pretty, brown-eyed Mrs. John Bricker's corsage was inscribed "from Ikey," a pet name from their courtship days; and on the Governor's desk in his office stood some "Better Times" roses marked "To John from your Abbie." The Governor leaned over his wife's chair to show her a diamond-set American Legion pin, presented that morning at the inaugural breakfast by the commander of the Ohio Department on behalf of the Legion men and women of the state. As he straightened up the "ready" signal came from the radio men.

His broad forehead serene with confidence, his eyes glowing with fearless purpose, Bricker faced the Chief Justice of the Ohio Supreme Court, raised his right hand, and repeated the oath which made him governor of the fourth most populous state in the Union.

As he waved to the cheering crowd and waited for the booming of the cannon to cease, he looked for his son and found the rail empty. Jack was down beside the cannon with the guardsmen. Halfway through the inaugural address, he clambered onto the rail again and fixed his attention on his father.

All Ohio was listening as the Governor promised, besides sound economical administration of the state's affairs, to oppose "with all the vitality we possess, the abuse of federal power when it means the destruction of local self-government within its proper sphere.

"There must be a revitalization of state and local governments through the nation," he declared. "The individual citizen must again be conscious of his responsibility to his government and alert to the preservation of his rights as a citizen under it. That cannot be done by taking government further away, but by keeping it at home.

"Here in America we are determined again to encourage business rather than to hinder it; to preserve opportunity and to recognize the proper place of the individual in his government.

"No superman or dictator can point the way to the better life we seek. It is a democratic task. The leadership must be of the many, of people of high character and good purpose. Such leadership is undramatic but safe. By it, democracies can serve and build."

The forty-five-year-old Governor left the cheering throng and walked into the office where Rutherford B. Hayes, William McKinley, Salmon P. Chase, Myron T. Herrick, Joseph B. Foraker, Judson Harmon, and James M. Cox had served Ohio before him.

Bricker had stipulated that his inauguration festivities must not cost the state a cent. "Don't spend any money you haven't got," he told the Chamber of Commerce committee in charge. Several weeks after the inauguration he discovered that there were unpaid bills amounting to $2,200. Instead of "passing the hat" he walked across the street and borrowed $2,200 on his personal note and paid off the bills.

The matter might have ended there if the Columbus newspapers had not carried the story. A hundred men, the Governor's personal friends, quietly contributed $22 each, and the bank canceled the note and returned it to the Governor. Occasionally a man with a silver "22" in his coat lapel can still be seen in Columbus—the badge of that group of Bricker's friends. It is typical of John Bricker that a hundred men would dig down in their pockets for him with no thought of political reward, and that he would know they had no such expectations.

CHAPTER IX

REORGANIZATION OF GOVERNMENT

IN THE PAST five years the government of Ohio has rendered more service to more people than ever before in the history of the state, while taking nothing away from private enterprise and keeping alive the processes of representative government. Governor Bricker and three Republican legislatures have written a record of improvement in all phases of the public's welfare. The history of Ohio's government during that time is living testimony to the falseness of the idea that representative government is clumsy, inefficient, and wasteful by its very nature. By choosing able men "of good purpose" for positions of responsibility, by initiating sound policies and carrying them out efficiently, he has shown that the traditional American way of government makes for the best government.

PERSONNEL IN THE NEW GOVERNMENT

The selection of his cabinet and other men in key positions was crucial to the success of Governor Bricker's plans for rehabilitating the state government. He had already outlined the standards he would apply in making appointments in his address to the Republican state convention. The patronage-hungry party leaders sat in the audience and heard their nominee list the specific questions he would ask about every prospective appointee:

"Is the appointee unbiased? There is no place for bigotry or narrowness in public office. Selfishness, prejudice, greed destroy representative government.

"Is he honest? No man should be appointed to public office who will compromise with his conscience for political gain. The strength of America is in the keeping of its trustworthy public officials.

"Is he a patriotic American? Subversive groups and influences abound in our land.

"Does the appointee know the job? Of the Republican committees, the first requirement I ask is that they recommend a competent man or woman. There are too many on the pay roll today who do not realize the real aims of our society or the purpose of our government.

"Will he work? There are thousands on the public pay roll of the nation and state today who, if they worked no harder in private employment than they do in public office, would be off the pay roll before tomorrow's sunrise.

"Finally, can he say 'No' to wrong? Too many in public office want to please every group, every clique, every faction. Honor and honesty say it cannot be done."

Party committeemen, he added, should ask these same questions about applicants for all patronage at their disposal.

Excellent campaign material, thought the party leaders, and went on laying plans to play politics as usual to make up for eight years out of power.

The "bosses" were not always pleased as the new governor's appointments were announced. They felt they were not having enough say; the Governor was not moving through channels; he was fulfilling his campaign promises literally. There were some indignant squawks from the "bosses," but Bricker continued to follow the course he had specifically charted. In time, with a few exceptions, the "bosses" came to see, with him, that the best politics to play is to give good government. Beginning with 1938, the Republican party in Ohio has had the greatest chain of successes in half a century.

And the people of Ohio noted that the men chosen by the Governor were experienced in fields related to their appointments; men whom the Governor had known, personally and in office, for a number of years; men who had ideas and the ability to put them into policy and action.

Second only to his passionate belief in the American representative government, Bricker's ability to select men of good judgment and high abilities has had most to do with the success of his administration as governor. He has never had to ask the resignation of a department head, nor to oust one. When a place falls vacant, he has found first-rate replacements, usually from experienced men within the administration.

A few of the most important of the appointments he made in 1939 will suffice to show the care with which he matched the job and the man.

BUDGET . REFORM

For the cabinet post of director of finance he chose William S. Evatt. Reform of the budget, a reconstruction of the whole financial set-up of the state, was one of the most important tasks confronting the new governor; and he chose a man who understood his point of view and was in sympathy with his aims —and who could say no with finality.

Evatt had been an attorney examiner in the state Division of Securities and chief counsel under Bricker and two other attorneys general, one of them a Democrat who had no other Republican on his staff. Ever since his appointment, Evatt has been one of the Governor's closest advisers. He is not a politician in the accepted sense; but his vision and political sense reach out much further than the "organization" angle of partisan groups.

Roars of laughter from the cabinet-meeting room are likely to mean that Evatt has been telling another of his lusty stories. He is a born raconteur, plays the violin, and does his own gardening; loves dogs and symphony music. On the job, however, he is a "tough guy"—tough in his language, hard to sway, inflexible in what he believes to be right.

The Constitution of Ohio provides that the state debt may not exceed $750,000 without a vote of the people. By some fiscal and legislative sleight-of-hand, however, Davey's government had circumvented this provision, and Bricker took over a state operating on a $40,000,000 deficit. It owed local school districts $18,000,000 which they had borrowed on the state's promise to pay at some later date, and on which the districts were paying interest. In the general revenue fund the deficit was $2,000,000; and $20,000,-000, four years' anticipated revenues from four special taxes for poor relief, had already been spent by the local subdivisions.

Bricker pledged his administration to put the state on a pay-as-you-go basis, retire the school debt as quickly as possible, provide adequate relief for the unemployed, meet the increased obligations of state aid for the aged, meet the full requirements of the state school financing program for the first time, start a long-overdue and sorely needed building program at welfare institutions, and maintain the regular day-to-day operations of the state government— all without any increase in taxes.

He proposed to do this in two ways: by reforming the budget, and by making the existing tax laws bring in the revenue they were intended to produce, by enforcing them thoroughly and uniformly. With this would go reduction in operating costs and hon-

97

est, efficient administration of all branches of government.

Public, politicians, and press alike were skeptical of this prodigious program. Most of them granted that the Governor would make a conscientious effort to do it; but they had no hope that he would succeed.

The Governor and Evatt began with two principal budget reforms: abolition of the general practice of earmarking taxes, and enactment of an all-inclusive general budget bill showing the taxpayers the exact total disbursements of state funds.

For a number of years the state had been trying to operate its diversified activities with a hodge-podge of earmarked taxes. Earmarking meant that when the legislature levied a special tax, it virtually wrote a blank check authorizing that the yield from that particular tax, whatever it turned out to be, should be spent for a specific purpose.

Bricker and his finance director found that earmarking can only work successfully when the cloth of expenditure is cut to the body of revenue. For instance, to earmark a gasoline tax for highway construction and maintenance is reasonable and feasible because the amount of fuel bought has a relationship to the number of miles of highway which can and should be built or kept up. If the yield from the gasoline tax is low, highway construction and repair can be trimmed to fit it. But it is nonsense to expect the expenditure for old-age pensions to match, say, the income from liquor taxes. It is nonsense to ask the public schools to build sound budgets when they depend partly on a percentage of the unknown yield of a retail sales tax and partly on the taxes collected from the sale of cigarettes.

At the beginning of 1939 the state's contributions to old-age pensions, poor relief, schools, and local governments all were made out of earmarked revenues. Naturally, cities, counties, and schools never knew how to construct their budgets. Furthermore, there could be no actual budgeting for poor relief. Sometimes as many as 37,000 old-age pensioners had to wait weeks for overdue checks because not enough funds from earmarked taxes had been collected to pay them. Of course, there was never any surplus from a year when the tax yield was good. The natural inclination of the tax-spenders was to use everything they got, whether they needed it or not, because it was theirs. As Governor Bricker expressed it:

"Earmarking provides a means for getting into debt, but no means of getting out. Under it, in good years all funds are spent; and in bad years the state's obligations pile up as a debt."

The legislature promptly responded to the Governor's recommendation by removing the earmarks from all taxes except fees for hunting and fishing licenses, which were set aside for conservation, and highway taxes. All other revenues went into one pool—the general revenue fund—and the legislature then made specific appropriations to meet the definite obligations of the state.

The all-inclusive budget bill for which the Governor asked was a daring innovation. He wanted a "comprehensive, clear, and honest bill which, instead of concealing, disclosed the real cost of government. . . . The people of Ohio are entitled to know just how much money their government is spending and the purposes for which it is expended."

When the budget reforms had been worked out and set in motion, Evatt was made tax commissioner; and R. R. Bangham, who as chairman of the House Finance Committee had steered them toward enactment, took his place. In 1940 Bingham resigned to seek an elective office, and the position of finance director was given to a man who knew budget building from the ground up, Herbert D. Defenbacher. He had been superintendent of the budget under both Evatt and Bangham, and for nearly four years now has directed the state's financial course with a success which the continuing economies and the treasury surplus clearly reflect.

DEPARTMENT OF TAXATION

Of all the department reorganizations, one of the most vital was the abolition of the old Tax Commission. Upon the Governor's recommendation the legislature abolished the Tax Commission and set up a tax commissioner charged with administration of all tax laws and a board of appeals, consisting of three members, each appointed for a six-year term.

This board performs the quasi-judicial function of reviewing orders of the commissioner upon appeal by interested parties. It is also the board of appeals from the action of county boards of review in fixing the value of local property for taxation.

Local government finances must have the approval of this board. A board of county affairs, under the board of appeals, has increased the efficiency of the laws providing revenue for local governments to the extent of millions of dollars annually.

By increasing the efficiency of audits and investigations into personal-property taxes, the Department of Taxation under Evatt has put thousands of new taxpayers on the rolls. The audits of large corporations with main offices outside Ohio have been especially productive. In the new Department of Taxation's first three and a half years, $7,000,000 were added to revenues for the benefit of local governments, in addition to increases in direct state subsidies and the allocations of state-collected revenues to the various subdivisions.

An improved system of auditing the returns from franchise taxes was largely responsible for collecting $1,500,000 in additional taxes from 1939 to 1942.

These improved tax laws and methods which brought in more revenue than before, were administered at a lower cost than formerly. Operating costs in the Department of Taxation were reduced more than $400,000 in the first year of Bricker's administration, and each succeeding year they have been

101

further decreased. The old Tax Commission had 860 employees; the Department of Taxation had 612 on July 1, 1943. Maintenance costs of the department have dropped 30 per cent.

The Cigarette Excise Tax Division shows a typical example of how costs were cut while revenues to the state were increased. For more than twelve years Ohio has collected a tax on cigarettes of two cents an average pack. The tax is collected through a stamp affixed to the pack, and the law provides a discount of not more than 10 per cent to wholesalers for putting on the stamps and canceling them. In 1939 Evatt discovered that the state had been allowing the full 10 per cent discount, whereas the actual cost to the wholesaler was slightly less than 5 per cent. He reduced the discount to 5 per cent, saving on an average more than $500,000 a year. By September 1, 1943, the saving had aggregated $2,054,602. In other words, in four years the state treasury received an additional $2,000,000 by following up one small administrative detail.

At the same time the Cigarette Excise Tax Division cut in half the cost of cigarette stamps by changing specifications to obtain competitive bidding. The state has been using far more stamps than in the past, yet saving $41,000 a year on the cost of them. In four years the aggregate saving on the printing of stamps has been $168,042.

As a means of enforcing the laws taxing securities, in 1941 corporations were required by act of legislature to file lists of stockholders with the Department of Taxation.

DEPARTMENT OF HIGHWAYS

To clean up the Highway Department, which spends over $30,000,000 a year, was a job for a man not only of proved integrity and business ability, but one who could enforce discipline as well. Bricker's choice for highway director was Lieutenant Colonel Robert S. Beightler, who was a veteran of the First World War and had had experience in the Highway Department as well as in running a contracting business. He served twenty months overseas with the Rainbow Division, and returned in 1918 to take a job in the Highway Department under Governor James M. Cox, Democrat. He went rapidly up the scale under another Democratic governor, Vic Donahey, and Myers Y. Cooper, a Republican. When he left the Highway Department and started a contracting business, he was chief engineer and assistant director of the department. When Bricker appointed him highway director, his firm switched its paving operations to another state.

In 1926 and 1927 Beightler attended the Army Command and General Staff School at Leavenworth; in 1931 he was graduated from the Army War College in Washington; and a year later he accepted duty with the War Plans Division. He took an active interest in the Ohio National Guard, and the Governor promoted him from colonel and chief of staff, to brigadier general, and finally to major general. When the Thirty-seventh Division of the National Guard went into federal service in 1940, Major General Beightler led them, first to Camp Shelby for training, and then to the Southwest Pacific. He and the Thirty-seventh went into action against the Japanese in the Solomons; and the New Georgia campaign brought him the Distinguished Service medal for outstanding leadership of his division in combat.

Beightler's knowledge, experience, and methods commanded respect from contractors and materials men; his qualities of leadership inspired loyalty in his subordinates and brought out their best efforts.

Highway Director Beightler broke the grasp of the "hot-mix" ring, and the paving material which had cost the state $12.96 per cubic yard was purchased for $8.00. In the first four years of the Bricker administration, Ohio constructed 630 miles of new highway, resurfaced and widened 3,197 miles, surface-treated 8,642 miles, and oiled 4,469 miles, at a total cost of $82,269,119.

This, and many added responsibilities arising out of war needs, was accomplished with fewer employees and at less cost in proportion to work done than under the previous administration.

Recent legislation, requested by Highway Director Hal G. Sours, authorizes him to keep the cost of estimates confidential until all bids are in. Director Sours moved up from assistant director when Beightler was called into service with the Army. He has done an able job in the department, shaping its activities and revising its plans to meet wartime conditions and evolving a comprehensive program of postwar construction.

DEPARTMENT OF LIQUOR CONTROL

The director of the Department of Liquor Control, an unlikely choice on the face of it, turned out to be an inspired one. Professor Jacob B. Taylor had been head of the Accountancy Department at Ohio State University. He had no experience in politics or the liquor business, which made public, politicians, and the liquor interests raise their collective eyebrows. When they discovered that the professor's middle name is Bacchus, there were good-natured gibes amid the wagging of heads.

Except for twenty-seven months as an army engineer in the First World War, most of them spent in France, Taylor had been a college professor all his life. He had written accounting textbooks, was at one time president of the American Accounting Association, and at the time of his appointment was a member of the board of directors of the Ohio Society of Certified Public Accountants. Further, he had supervised the installation of the accounting system in the Department of Liquor Control in 1934 and had kept in touch with it ever since.

As director of the department, he brought a new

approach and new methods to one of the most vital activities of the state. He cracked down on "rake-off" and "shake-down" practices immediately, and the department was operated without a trace of scandal for the four years of his incumbency. Economy, increased profits and revenues, and law enforcement reached impressive levels.

One of the first acts of the new department was to cancel its contract with the truckless trucking company. Attorney General Thomas J. Herbert, who had served as special counsel under Bricker, recovered $113,740 of excess payments from the bogus company.

This company had sublet its contract at 11½ cents a case out of the 17 cents it received. The Department of Liquor Control let its contract to a genuine trucking company at 10½ cents a case, saving an additional $20,000 a year. The cost of operating the department was reduced $875,000 a year, and the net yield to the state treasury from liquor in 1939-1940 was $4,350,000 more than in 1937-1938.

Throughout the Bricker administration, the only criticism of the Liquor Control Department has been criticism of the shortage of stock resulting from wartime curtailment of production. A monopoly state is not in a position to build up large inventories, and therefore the liquor shelves were nearly empty early in 1943. The legislature instituted a rationing program which has operated smoothly and satisfactorily in general.

Director of public welfare in Ohio is a tremendous and difficult job. He administers not only twenty-three huge welfare, health, reform, and penal institutions, but also the programs of public assistance. The Governor intended also to add to his duties the administration of unemployment relief.

Charles L. Sherwood, who became director of public welfare, had behind him an exceptional combination of political and public-welfare activities. He started his political career as a county committeeman, successfully managed Theodore E. Burton's campaign for United States Senator in 1928, was assistant state welfare director from 1929 to 1931, and in the latter year was named executive secretary of the Ohio Mental Hygiene Association. He had also been a staff member of the Ohio Institute, a governmental research organization, and had engaged in a variety of welfare activities, including membership on the White House Committee on Child Welfare in 1931.

A man of unusual determination, he did what he saw needed to be done, without explanation to anyone except the Governor and those directly involved. He sometimes brought on himself sharp criticism from press and public; but in the long run they both realized that Sherwood's acts resulted in improved conditions at the various institutions. He was exactly the kind of man needed to tighten up the loose ad-

107

ministration of unemployment relief. In time, local relief authorities learned to work amicably with the state welfare director, and together they solved problems which had been sources of friction for many years. Eventually the result was a smoother administration of adequate relief at less cost to the taxpayers.

One of Sherwood's first jobs was cleaning up the Ohio penitentiary, where a lax administration had left a sordid state of affairs. With the Governor's approval, Sherwood ousted the warden and put in charge a noted penologist, W. F. Amrine, who had resigned as superintendent of the state prison farm when Governor Davey ordered him to investigate and report on the political affiliation of each farm employee. Eventually Brigadier General Frank D. Henderson, of the Ohio National Guard, was appointed warden of the penitentiary, and Amrine went back to superintending the prison farm.

The new warden was a Democrat who had been adjutant general for ten years under two Democratic governors, Donahey and White. His selection angered the Republican politicians of the state, and they were a long time getting over it; but before long his merits became apparent.

Henderson had been one of the best adjutant generals in Ohio history. Besides the usual functions of his office he had taken on such unusual duties as administrating relief to the families of unemployed miners during the prolonged labor disputes of the

1920's, organizing drought relief in the early 1930's, and organizing the first state unemployment-relief set-up in 1932. Subsequently he became the state's first relief administrator, and then successively the director of the CWA and the FERA in Ohio.

He is a disciplinarian with a brusque manner, but by no means a martinet. He was noted for fair and just decisions, and in retrospect appears to have been an ideal selection to manage one of the largest prisons in the country. For twenty-five years the Ohio penitentiary had rocked with scandals and threats of scandal. In 1930 it suffered one of the worst fires in history, which court testimony established had been set by prisoners.

Warden Henderson established a school for guards and brought in experts to train them. He set up a classification board to discover each prisoner's aptitudes and give him a corresponding institutional assignment. A department of industrial arts was established, soon turning out more than a hundred different articles. The warden reorganized the prison court which tried and punished unruly prisoners. He set up a board to recommend prisoners for transfer to the prison farm. He established a dental clinic which in its first seven months treated 4,800 patients and made and fitted 462 sets of false teeth. A new optical department in one month's time fitted 606 prisoners with spectacles which had been donated, reconditioned, or purchased at wholesale. These reforms ended the plague of periodic crises which had kept the prison in a ferment for years.

In the first year of the new administration, $750,-000 was set aside for a building program for state welfare institutions. By 1942 the amount had increased to $4,375,000. Despite wartime prices and an increased number of state wards, the appropriation for maintenance of state institutions was raised $1,900,000 in the fourth year of Bricker's administration.

In administering its twenty-three institutions, the Department of Public Welfare adopted business practices which saved the state several millions of dollars in the purchase of food, fuel, and other supplies. About a million dollars' worth of foodstuffs—one-third of the annual food bill—is now grown on institutional farms each year.

Employment of modern methods in the treatment of mental cases has resulted in increasing the recovery rate to over 50 per cent of the new patients admitted to all state hospitals. The Commission for the Blind has provided more surgical operations and raised the resulting incidence of improved vision from 45.5 per cent in 1940 to 96 per cent in 1942. On an average, 275 blind persons are receiving vocational training to fit them for useful occupations.

In 1943 Sherwood resigned as director to become chairman of the Pardon and Parole Commission. His successor is Herbert R. Mooney, his former assistant director.

In reorganizing the Department of Health, the legislature provided for a state director of health appointed to a five-year term by the governor from a list of qualified persons submitted by the Public Health Council. The Governor named Dr. Roll H. Markwith, health commissioner in Akron, to head the department, and the Public Health Council confirmed his choice. With a wide training in public health behind him, Dr. Markwith has given the state an effective administration.

During Bricker's administration, the Department of Health has extended public-health service to rural areas in the shape of financial assistance and advice, so that each of the 204 health districts in the state now employs a local health commissioner. Fully equipped dental trailers help local officials and schools in conducting dental-health education programs.

The Health Department has helped set up free venereal clinics and provides free antisyphilitics to physicians. The legislature has established medical service associations to provide doctors' care for lower-income groups. Laws have been passed to regulate the marketing of milk and to license livestock dealers.

DIVISION OF AID FOR THE AGED

Thomas W. McCaw, a successful businessman, who had served overseas as an artillery captain in the

111

First World War, became the first director of the Division of Aid for the Aged under Bricker. He left to rejoin the Army in the present war, and Karl R. Babb, his assistant for three years, took his place.

When Governor Bricker took office, there were 111,188 persons on the old-age pension rolls entitled to receive monthly aid checks, and the average check in the month of highest payment had been $22.58. Sometimes checks failed to appear for weeks because there was no money to pay them, and 20,000 applications were on file awaiting action by the state.

Within a year and a half, 16,300 additional pensioners were receiving checks in Ohio. The average check was $22.86; checks were received on time; all of the inherited 20,000 applications had been passed upon; and new applications were receiving quick action.

At a special session of the legislature called by Governor Bricker in June 1940, the maximum for old-age payments was raised, effective January 1, 1941, from the $30-a-month provision in the law adopted by the voters in 1933 to the $40 provided in the revised federal Social Security Act.

In January 1942, the number of pensioners reached the all-time high of 135,567, and the average check was $26.98. Improved economic conditions then began to be reflected in reduced pension rolls.

In September 1943, the number of old-age pensioners was 132,342, of whom 50,000 received $30 or more a month and 5,000 received the $40 maximum.

The average monthly check was $27.66, an increase of $5.00 a month in four years. As compared with 20,000 on the waiting list when Bricker went into office, only 3,222 applicants were waiting in the fall of 1943. The cost of administering the Division of Aid for the Aged was less in each of the first four years of the Bricker administration than in the last year of the preceding administration. The state's lien on property of old-age pensioners had been abolished by legislative act.

DEPARTMENT OF EDUCATION

Keeping the Republican platform pledge, the legislature submitted to the voters an amendment to establish a state board of education with authority to choose the state director of education, instead of his being appointed by the governor. This amendment was swamped in a general avalanche of negative votes which defeated several proposals submitted to the electorate in 1939, including a "ham-and-eggs" proposal for old-age pensions.

The administration more than fulfilled its pledge to wipe out the public-school debt. At the end of the first year of Bricker's administration, $3,000,000 was paid off, and the state had taken over the interest payments on the remainder, thus giving $250,000 more relief to local school districts. In addition, the state met the full requirements of the school financing program for the first time, contributing $7,000,-

113

ooo a year more in direct subsidies to local school districts than in any previous year and making payments each time they came due. Early in the fifth year of the administration, the $18,000,000 school debt had been paid off completely.

An appropriation of $2,317,000 was made in 1941 for a building program in the state universities, and their personal and maintenance item was increased by $700,000. The universities' building appropriation has since been substantially increased. A fund for rehabilitation of public-school buildings in needy districts was set up by the legislature, which also established indefinite tenure for schoolteachers and authorized the Department of Education to set up a training program for handicapped children.

The director named to the department was Kenneth C. Ray, a former state legislator and superintendent of public schools in Zanesville.

DIVISION OF SECURITIES

The Division of Securities estimates that various kinds of rackets defrauded investors of $25,000,000 in 1934-1938. By vigorous prosecution of ringleaders, the division has virtually eliminated from Ohio the whisky-warehouse racket, the cemetery-lot-sale racket, and the passbook-company racket.

Small loan companies have been placed under stricter regulation; the rate of interest they are allowed to return has been reduced. Illegal loan-shark

114

operators—pay-roll lenders who prey on wage earners —have been eliminated.

The Division of Securities limited the expansion of note issues by private corporations, thus protecting the investors and allowing the corporations to stay in business despite wartime restrictions on credit buying.

The chief of the division is Paul L. Selby, a personal friend and college mate of the Governor's, and formerly an assistant attorney general.

DIVISION OF INSURANCE

The Governor appointed as superintendent of insurance John A. Lloyd, formerly a state senator and secretary of the Ohio Division of Insurance Agents. When he resigned to take a position in private business, he was succeeded by the deputy superintendent, J. Roth Crabbe, once an assistant attorney general under Bricker.

The Division of Insurance sponsored legislation giving it authority to police bond investment companies and to drive out of the state firms which fail to keep on deposit with the Superintendent of Insurance the entire cash surrender value of all outstanding contracts.

DEPARTMENT OF COMMERCE

To the Department of Commerce the Governor named Charles H. Jones, formerly an assistant attorney general, and before that Republican floor-leader in the Ohio House of Representatives and one of the ablest legislators of the last twenty years.

Aggressive supervision of banks under Governor Bricker has eliminated from their books over $23,000,000 of substandard bonds and over $20,000,000 of real estate acquired from debtors. During the first four years of the Bricker administration, the assets of state banks increased 48 per cent and totaled approximately $2,500,000,000 at the end of 1942.

Ohio has the greatest volume of building-and-loan assets of any state in the Union. The Bricker administration found that in many of the liquidations incident to the depression, large sums which should have been returned to investors were frozen by the directors, ostensibly for reorganization purposes. It found assets being dissipated and stock transfers juggled for the benefit of directors. There was evidence of a fictitious market for the purchase of stock from distressed owners.

After long, bitter court battles, the Department of Commerce took over the liquidation of the loan companies, with the result that liquidation costs were reduced, frozen money was thawed out and distributed to the depositors and stockholders.

REORGANIZATION BY LEGISLATIVE ACT

In some important instances, the Governor soon learned, the appointment of new department heads was not enough to carry through his plans for reorganization. If improvements were to be made with any reasonable speed or lasting effect, complete reorganization by legislative act was required. There were some cases in which his hands would be tied for months to come unless the legislature boldly cut the cords.

The outgoing Governor Davey had packed his own appointees into several important boards and commissions which would carry over into Bricker's administration. An outgoing "lame-duck" General Assembly had given senate confirmation to these appointments with its last gasp of life. Bricker saw at once that the appointments were made for the express purpose of continuing certain policies of the discredited retiring administration and keeping hundreds of its adherents in the department personnel. There were literally thousands of government employees who had escaped civil service by one means or another, mostly the state's failure to give examinations for the classified service. By retaining close political control of certain governing boards and commissions, it would be possible to keep these Davey satellites on the state pay roll for years.

To prevent this, the Governor asked the legislature to abolish several existing commissions and boards, replacing them with new departments. In most instances the proposed reorganizations included redefinition of authority and recodification of the laws pertaining to and administered by the department in question.

At once the cry of "Ripper!" was raised, and for a while there was considerable opposition to the reorganization bills. Both the Governor and the legislature, however, believed they had a clear mandate from the voters. In the election the public had expressed itself forcefully on the need for a change. Throughout his administration Bricker has had behind him a predominantly Republican legislature, loyal but not subservient. Governor and legislature set to work with the tools of government available to repair the damage Davey had done.

BUREAU OF UNEMPLOYMENT COMPENSATION

Bricker estimated that the Unemployment Compensation Commission had been overloaded by probably 25 per cent. The *Ohio State Journal* described the commission as a "political dumping ground." At a midnight session, in its last moments of life, the outgoing Senate had confirmed the appointment of Keith Lawrence, who had been Davey administration leader in the Senate, to a six-year term on the commission.

The legislature under Bricker abolished the commission and replaced it with the Bureau of Unemployment Compensation, in which an administrator and a three-member board of review took over respectively the administrative and quasi-judicial duties

118

of the cumbersome commission. Lawrence went out with the commission, but the other two commission members, one a Republican and one a Democrat, were named to the new board of review. Verner E. Metcalf, who as senator was the spark plug of the legislative investigation of the Davey regime, became the new Republican member.

The administrator of the new bureau was Herschel C. Atkinson, a former newspaperman and at the time an executive in the Akron Chamber of Commerce. Atkinson proved a diligent administrator, and in 1941 and 1942 he led the unemployment-insurance departments of the various states in their fight against the federal government's bureaucratic attempts to federalize the compensation departments.

In the first few months of the Bricker administration, the proportion of civil-service employees in the Bureau of Unemployment Compensation increased from 55 per cent to 96 per cent, and Ohio's administration of unemployment compensation established one of the best records for efficiency and economy in all the states.

Legislation in the Bricker administration has liberalized the unemployment-compensation law to such an extent that jobless Ohioans in 1942 received $2,700,000 more in benefits than they would have received under the old law. At the same time it has established merit rating for Ohio employers, saving them $50,000,000 in contributions, while providing the unemployment-compensation fund with $44,000,-

ooo in 1942—more than three times the amount required that year for the payment of benefits. Recently, however, insurance rates in the mushroom war industries have been increased in order to help build a surplus in the compensation fund against the expected recession in the wake of the war. On September 30, 1943, Ohio had $319,226,588 in unemployment-compensation contributions to its credit in the trust fund in Washington.

INDUSTRIAL COMMISSION

Workmen's compensation has been liberalized further in the Bricker administration than at any time in the twenty-five years before 1939; partly through legislative enactment and partly through new administrative policies and efficient operation. Within the first year, 10,000 employers who had escaped participation in the workmen's-compensation system were brought under its terms, giving protection to 80,000 additional workers. Virtually all occupational diseases have been given coverage by the law. The powers and duties of the regional boards of the Industrial Commission have been more clearly defined to make workable and efficient a set-up designed to provide hearings close to the homes of injured workmen and other claimants, and to speed up settlements.

By act of legislature, death awards under workmen's compensation have been increased from $6,500 to $7,000; the maximum award for partial disability from $4,000 to $6,000; and the maximum award for temporary disability from $3,750 to $4,200. The increase in death awards was the first in seventeen years; that in disability awards, the first in ten years.

While increasing benefits to the workmen, the Industrial Commission at the same time has made the most substantial reduction in many years in insurance rates assessed against employers. On July 1, 1940, it ordered a 9.4 per cent reduction in the general level of rates; in 1941, a further reduction of 3.2 per cent; in 1942, an additional cut of 10.2 per cent; and in 1943 another 8 per cent.

The handling of claims was expedited in the first few months under Bricker so that the time between receipt of an ordinary claim and payment was reduced one-half.

Meanwhile, despite the reduced premiums and substantially increased benefits, Ohio's workmen's-compensation fund was the first in the nation to pass the $100,000,000 mark. On October 1, 1943, she had invested in federal government bonds $64,534,300 of this amount as one of her contributions to the war.

DEPARTMENT OF INDUSTRIAL RELATIONS

The minimum-wage law has been rigidly enforced and its application extended under George A. Stain, director of the Department of Industrial Relations. Before wages climbed with production, the department collected in a year nearly twice as much in back wages for underpaid women employees as had been collected in the five years preceding. Just recently a law was passed relaxing the restrictions on the employment of women and minors in war industries and other essential and collateral occupations.

Vocational education is provided for injured workmen as soon as they are physically fit for it, through co-operation between the Department of Industrial Relations and the Department of Education. Artificial limbs and appliances are provided when necessary, and a $10 weekly maintenance is paid to the workman while he is taking a rehabilitation course. In 1942 the rehabilitation of adults was more than twice what it was in 1939. A similar program has been worked out with the Red Cross for the rehabilitation of injured men returning from the war.

THE ADJUTANT GENERAL

The Davey administration had secured a life-tenure law for the Adjutant General of Ohio, the commanding officer of the Ohio National Guard. The law probably was unconstitutional, in that it would have deprived the governor, the constitutional commander in chief of the national guard, of the power to appoint his top officers, a situation which would leave the way open for partisan politics to flare up in this important branch of the state government to interfere with the enforcement of order in a crisis.

At Governor Bricker's request, the legislature repealed the life-tenure law and re-established the governor's right to name his own adjutant general.

Under Major General Gilson D. Light, Governor Bricker's first choice, the Ohio National Guard was kept at a high level of efficiency. In the fall of 1940 it was mustered into federal army service as the Thirty-seventh Division, one of the best-prepared national guard organizations in the country. Shortly before his death early in 1941, General Light established Ohio's selective service machinery, which has since functioned to the entire satisfaction of the federal selective service administration under other former Ohio National Guard officers, headed by Colonel Chester W. Goble. Lieutenant Colonel Whittier S. Bird, chief of staff of the Thirty-seventh Division, became adjutant general; when he rejoined the Thirty-seventh in the South Pacific, Brigadier General Donald F. Pancoast, of the Ohio State Guard, long an officer of the National Guard and a veteran of overseas service in World War I, became adjutant general.

COMMISSION OF PARDON AND PAROLE

At the conclusion of his term, Davey made his secretary, Myrna Smith, a member of the Board of Parole for a term of three years and seven months.

This was too obviously an attempt to continue control of the board by an administration already repudiated. The new legislature followed the Governor's request and replaced the Parole Board with a Commission of Pardon and Parole, with redefined powers, at the same time improving the clemency laws of the state.

The governor's position as the last appeal for a condemned man is a difficult one for any man, and John Bricker takes it hard. Shortly after he became governor, a convicted murderer appealed to him for clemency, with execution only a few hours away. Bricker could find no extenuating circumstances in the case and refused the appeal. As far as anyone could see, he did not flinch. As the lawyer and the murderer's relatives were ushered out the door, a state employee came in. The office seemed to be empty, but as the door was closed from outside, the Governor was revealed behind it, a rumpled handkerchief in his hand, his eyes red. He said nothing, and his visitor made no reference to it.

CIVIL SERVICE COMMISSION

The state Civil Service Commission needed a complete revamping—new funds with which to conduct competitive examinations, but also new blood in its personnel and a reorganization of its function. Provisional and temporary employees who had never competed for their jobs, badly needed weeding out.

For a number of years the commission had been a two-member board—one Democrat and one Republican—a set-up which Governor Bricker thought divided responsibility and opened up too much opportunity for log-rolling, back-scratching, and stalemates. During his campaign he had advocated a three-member commission, the effective administration of which would belong to the party in power. Accordingly, he proposed such a bill to the legislature and it passed it; but the Democratic state organization sponsored a referendum on the act. The bill was smothered in the same vote directed against radical pension legislation which also killed the Board of Education reorganization amendment.

Despite the rejection of his reorganization plan, the Governor managed to give the Civil Service Commission new life by appointing Gertrude Jones to the chairmanship. Miss Jones, who had once missed election to Congress by only a few votes in a strongly Democratic year, directed her talents toward bringing order into the civil-service system. Behind her she had the largest appropriation in the state's history for the conduct of competitive examinations.

During the first eight months of her chairmanship, the commission examined 18,000 persons for state jobs. The provisional and temporary appointees were replaced with the successful applicants, and a backlog of competent aspirants was established. By the end of 1942, examinations had been given to 43,000 applicants for state jobs.

125

Where lack of eligible lists necessitates provisional appointments, noncompetitive examinations are now given to prevent employment of unqualified persons. Eight thousand jobs not formerly classified have been classified, and 9,000 ratings have been advanced to give equal ratings and salaries to employees doing the same work.

The Civil Service Commission has established more direct supervision over the 114 municipal commissioners. The legislature has provided a credit bonus for veterans of the Second World War who take civil-service examinations, and has provided for them to receive special preference.

DEPARTMENT OF AGRICULTURE

Under an act of the legislature passed in the first year of the Bricker administration, the Department of Agriculture started a Bangs-disease eradication program. With $700,000 in state funds, matched by federal money, more than 2,500,000 head of cattle were tested for Bangs disease and bovine tuberculosis in the first four years of his administration. An additional $253,000 was provided in the 1943-1944 budget. This program has saved the dairy industry in Ohio and made it possible to keep the state's high standing as a source for foundation herds of pure-bred cattle.

An energetic campaign has been waged against the Japanese beetle.

A milk-marketing administration, established within the Division of Foods and Dairies, licensed personnel in the industry for competency, stabilized milk prices, and restored financial solvency to thousands of dealers. Operation of farmers' co-operatives also has been liberalized by legislation.

In 1941 the legislature authorized the establishment of soil-conservation districts and county-wide districts have been set up in twelve counties, following hearings of petitioners.

The Ohio Agricultural Experiment Station has been provided with expanded facilities under the Bricker administration. It has developed a new variety of wheat which has produced 62 bushels to the acre, with a potential increased yield of $5,000,000 a year to Ohio farmers. The station has also developed hybrid corn varieties of 30 per cent greater yield, and other hybrids almost wholly resistant to the corn borer. Use of these varieties is credited with increasing Ohio's corn crop 22,000,000 bushels in 1942 over 1941. Through experiments in sugar-beet culture, an increase of 4 tons per acre, or 200,000 tons a year, has been made possible.

Experiments in the cross-breeding of beef cattle developed a strain which averages 45 pounds heavier at 7 months than the average pure-bred strain. If the results of these experiments were put into general practice, 25,000,000 pounds would be added to Ohio's production of beef and veal. Crossbreeding of hogs and the development of new breeds of sheep are producing increased yields also. Soil experiments have been successful in producing good yields of corn on virgin soil and raw subsoil.

Early in his administration, Governor Bricker named a state Chemurgic Committee which co-operates with the national Chemurgic Council in developing new commercial uses for products of the soil.

The Ohio Water Supply Board, established by the legislature in 1941, has taken steps to conserve and replenish the supplies of water, both underground and surface, for agricultural, industrial, and public use.

The Director of Agriculture is John T. Brown, farmer and former lieutenant governor of Ohio. The department's energetic assistant director is Mrs. Lottie M. Randolph, who had been identified with farm activities for many years and holds the title of Master Home Maker, which corresponds in the woman's field to Master Farmer, a title held by her late husband.

DIVISION OF CONSERVATION AND NATURAL RESOURCES

The new Division of Conservation and Natural Resources is governed by a bi-partisan commission appointed by the governor and financed by the revenue from hunting and fishing licenses. The commission selects the conservation commissioner and his assistants; all other employees are civil-service appointees. In his first year as governor, Bricker appointed Don Waters, Sandusky sportsman, as commissioner of conservation. When the new commission was created, it ratified the selection by naming Waters.

Seven district conservation offices have been opened in various parts of the state; and in each of the 88 counties are conservation committees composed of farmer and sportsman members selected by their own groups. These committees meet with the Conservation and Natural Resources Commission to advise upon the opinions of farmers and sportsmen on fish and game regulations.

The commission has inaugurated the teaching of conservation in public schools; increased the acreage of inland lakes and parks by 50 per cent; thrown open 100,000 acres of state forest to hunting by adopting controlled hunting methods; adopted a plan of headwater reservoirs for the natural propagation of fish; and has established new records for the release of game and fish for the pleasure of hunters and fishers.

OTHER DEPARTMENTAL ACCOMPLISHMENTS

The state Fire Marshal's Division, under Marshal Ray R. Gill, a former division chief recalled to his post by Governor Bricker at the beginning of his administration, has increased the number of building inspections and correctional orders to a point where

129

Ohio now has the lowest average insurance rates of any state. More effective administration of the licensing laws under the Fire Marshal increased the revenues from restaurant licenses 17.5 per cent, and from dry-cleaning establishments 12.2 per cent between 1939 and 1943, as compared with the preceding administration. The job was done with greatly decreased personnel.

By a campaign of truck inspection, the Bureau of Motor Vehicles has collected $950,000 in fines and license violations. Throughout the administration, the bureau has been headed by Cylon W. Wallace, a Toledo businessman.

During Bricker's first year as governor, the prosecution of pure-food-law violators increased 45 per cent, and the collection of fines 275 per cent.

The Public Works Department, under Frank L. Raschig of Cincinnati, has increased the revenues obtained by the state from industrial uses of canal lands and waters, and has efficiently operated and maintained the state's buildings and other properties.

MISCELLANEOUS LEGISLATION

The first legislature under Bricker's administration required municipalities to maintain a fireman's pension fund. To break log jams on needed railroad-crossing elimination, it reduced the percentage of cost borne by the railroads. It stipulated that peace officers using motor vehicles in making arrests must wear distinctive uniforms and use only cars or motor-cycles distinctively marked. To end joy-riding in state automobiles, a law was passed requiring state cars to be plainly labeled.

One of several purposes for which Governor Bricker called the legislature into special session in 1940 was the separation of the national and state ballots. As Bricker went into his 1940 campaign for re-election, he recalled the use Davey had made of the single-ballot situation in 1936. Now, he was fac-ing Davey again and he had no fear what the result would be if a clear expression could be obtained from the voters on the issues affecting state govern-ment. In his message to the special session, he said:

"The issues of the national campaign are changing hourly. International relations are acute and their consideration and discussion is paramount. I am bound by ties of loyalty to my party. I devoutly be-lieve in the two-party system of government as the only method of making real representative govern-ment work. I know you of both parties share that feeling.

"I also recognize that a great group of our finest citizens are not so bound, and their desire to serve and their interests in government are just as real and as sincere as yours and mine.

"This year of all years, there is reason for the sepa-ration of the ballots. A former governor, with a record, has been nominated on the other ticket. . . . The issues should be clear cut. I have an abiding confidence in the judgment of the voters. By separating the ballots, we get a free expression of that judgment.

"This bill should be passed as an emergency act. In doing so you will not be depriving the people of Ohio of a vote on any public policy, but rather give them a fair chance to say what they think of the past administration and this one. This action will bring Ohio in line with practically every other state in the Union."

The special session of the legislature acted speedily, and the separation of the ballots was an accomplished fact on the eve of the national conventions.

The General Assembly of 1941, besides taking steps to provide for the defense of the state in the face of possible emergency, enacted a uniform traffic code, recodified the juvenile and probate court statutes, authorized establishment of soil-conservation districts, enacted a new mine safety code, put the employees of city health districts under civil service, and made examination for venereal disease compulsory before marriage licenses could be issued.

In 1943, the General Assembly passed a bill providing uniform procedure by the various licensing agencies of the state, for hearings on their acts with regard to licenses and a uniform appeal to the common pleas courts from the actions of licensing boards or agents. This bill, particularly recommended by Governor Bricker, is one of the most important legislative accomplishments in Ohio in many years.

An Informal Speech

The same legislature abolished virtually the last remnants of the fee system of compensation for public officials in Ohio. The fees paid to county commissioners above their fixed salaries for inspection of ditches and sewers have been abolished, the fees allowed probate judges in inheritance-tax cases have been done away with, and the judges are now exclusively on fixed salaries.

At the instance of a strong farm bloc, the legislature of 1943 passed a bill to move Ohio's clocks back an hour from Eastern War Time, and the Governor approved the bill.

A stronger law against gambling, making second offenses punishable with prison terms, is designed to get rid of the numbers or policy racket.

The same legislature required public utilities corporations to make increased contributions for the maintenance of the Public Utilities Commission. It established commissions for: studying the problems of the small businessman; making plans for the postwar period; acquiring sites and planning the construction of the new state schools for the deaf and the blind; and continuing the study of administrative procedure.

CHAPTER X

ECONOMIES LARGE AND SMALL

THE GOVERNOR did not wait to get the state's book-keeping reformed before starting the economy program he had promised. During his first five days he dropped 1,047 employees from the pay roll; at the end of ten days the number of dismissals had risen to 1,319; and at the end of three weeks to 2,199.

Firing superfluous employees was far from the only move for economy. Department heads were instructed to economize every chance they saw, no matter how small the item. The first bill passed by the legislature, the temporary budget bill, carried an antigraft clause. Early in the campaign of 1938, Bricker had said:

"I shall recommend the enactment of a statute requiring that all persons, firms, and individuals selling goods to the state of Ohio shall, as a condition of receiving any business from the state, furnish satisfactory proof that no 'commissions' have been or will be paid to any political 'fixer' to obtain such business."

The antigraft clause was his prompt fulfillment of that promise, and it was later expanded into a permanent law, providing penalties for any person found guilty of collusion in securing contracts. The era of good pickings was over.

Department heads found one economy after another, and they mounted up into substantial savings. The president of the Citizens' Tax League of Ohio, S. P. Bush, a Democrat, was moved to remark:

"This is the first time in my forty-eight years of personal observation that I have seen a governor of Ohio actually roll up his sleeves and start saving the people's money."

The state purchasing agent found that coal could be bought 15 to 25 cents a ton cheaper than the price the previous administration had been paying, and the coal bill for the state's huge welfare institutions was thus reduced $200,000 a year. The food bill for the 23,000 persons cared for in welfare institutions offered one small economy after another. Coffee was bought at 2 cents a pound less than the state had been paying, milk at 2 cents a gallon less, and tobacco at 2 cents a pound less. The price of corn syrup in the state's institutional budget dropped from 40 cents to 30 cents a gallon; pea beans from $7.42 to $2.99 a hundredweight; bacon from $16.24 to $9.37 a hundredweight; prunes from 6.7 cents to 3.6 cents a pound; raisins from 9.2 cents to 5.2 cents a pound. In all, the purchasing agent saved the state $845,000 in such supplies during the first year of Bricker's administration.

In the Department of Liquor Control, trucking

costs were cut $169,000 for the year; the cost of warehousing for the liquor was reduced $92,000; and rentals for state stores went down $160,000 through more advantageous leases or moving to less expensive locations. Traveling expenses in the department were cut $125,000, and its administrative expenses alone were cut more than a fifth, a reduction of $1,900,000 in the two years of 1939 and 1940, as compared with the preceding two-year period.

In the Highway Department a saving of $216,510 was made in the purchase of oil, asphalt, and tar; the cost of construction of one type of "hot-mix" road was cut $19,000 per mile; and salaries in the department were over a million dollars less than in 1938.

The Governor named a full-time salvage supervisor to salvage any materials, supplies, equipment, or machinery which one institution or department could no longer use and assign it to some other state activity which needed it. Actual scrap and waste materials were to be sold for the highest price obtainable. This program was instituted more than two years before the nation became scrap-conscious under the impetus of wartime scarcity.

Under the new warden, prisoners of the Ohio penitentiary salvaged scrap metals which brought $4,000 on the market. Within three and half years, the salvage program throughout state departments and institutions netted $120,000 and saved the state an additional $38,000 in transferred equipment.

At the end of his first year as governor, Bricker's record was one of achievement on every point in the fiscal program he had mapped out:

The state had been put on a pay-as-you-go basis; deficit financing had been stopped.

The state had paid $3,000,000 on the public-school debt and taken over full responsibility for paying off the interest on the remaining notes, a saving to the local school districts of another $250,000.

The state had contributed $1,000,000 more for poor relief than in the previous year, at the same time enforcing economies in local relief administration by disabusing local governments of the idea that state money was "easy money."

The state had met increased old-age-pension obligations to the extent of $1,700,000 above the last year's contributions.

The state had met the full requirements of the school financing program for the first time, contributing $7,000,000 more in direct subsidies to the local school districts than had been paid in the previous year, and making payments each time as they were due.

A $750,000 building program had been started at the state's welfare institutions—a mere dent in the needs, but a beginning.

The regular day-to-day operations of the state government had been maintained at a saving of $5,150,-000 in personal-service and maintenance costs.

There was a net surplus of $3,369,268 in the state

treasury. And there had been no increase in taxes.

During Bricker's second year as governor, the state contributed $16,320,000 more in subsidies for the public schools, poor relief, and old-age pensions than it had in the last year of Davey's administration, and another $3,000,000 of the school debt was paid off. Despite these increased contributions, the unencumbered balance in the general revenue fund grew to $6,435,277—nearly double the balance at the end of the first year.

There were no new or increased taxes back of these achievements. What made them possible was that the cost of the normal operations of the state government had been cut more than $20,000,000 in the two years, as compared with the preceding biennium; and along with the saving went a higher level of efficiency in the day-to-day operation of the government.

The economies of Governor Bricker's first term continued through his second, and, with the help of increased revenues owing to improved business conditions in 1941 and 1942, accomplished the following major improvements in state finances:

The public-school debt was reduced another $6,000,000, leaving only $6,000,000 to be paid of the $18,000,000 debt inherited on January 1, 1939.

Old-age-pension payments were increased $12,857,-484 over those of 1939-1940. This was done to give aid to additional needy old people, to meet increased living costs, and to make possible the maximum payment, raised from $30 to $40 in 1940.

To meet higher market prices and the needs of a larger number of state wards, the appropriation for the maintenance of state welfare institutions was increased $1,900,000. At the Governor's request, the legislature set aside $4,375,000 for a building program in these institutions, and another $2,517,000 for a similar program in the six state universities—an amount which could be met almost entirely out of the net surplus in the treasury at the end of his first term. Also, the personal-service and maintenance item for the state universities was increased $700,000.

The Industrial Commission's appropriation was raised $350,000 to take care of the increased work of the department. Under stricter enforcement of the workmen's-compensation laws, 10,000 additional employers had been brought within their scope during 1939-1940, providing protection for more working people than ever before in the state's history.

The treasury surplus at the end of Bricker's second term was $41,570,176, not including some $4,000,000 of the fund for new institutional buildings which the state had not been able to start because of the curtailment of materials and priorities resulting from the war.

In 1943, at the Governor's request, the legislature reappropriated the $4,000,000 building fund and added another $13,000,000 for a postwar building program to provide the state with welfare and educational buildings it has been needing for thirty years, and incidentally will provide a cushion against postwar unemployment. New state schools for the blind and deaf are included in the program.

Out of the surplus, also, the state was able to liquidate, two years ahead of time, the remaining $6,000,000 of the school debt.

The renovation of government finances which Bricker accomplished—one of the political marvels of this century—was not confined to the state budget. Local governments throughout the state have benefited, both in increased direct subsidies from the state and in taxes collected by the state and shared with the local governments. Each year during the Bricker administration, the state has paid $1,000,000 more in direct subsidies to local governments than in 1938; but the state contribution for poor relief has been gradually decreased with increasing employment. The local share of state-collected taxes was $6,750,000 more during Bricker's first two years than in 1937-1938; in his second term it was $12,850,000 more than in 1937-1938, an advance of $6,100,000 over the record of his first term.

This increase in the amount of taxes was to some extent due to improved business conditions, but largely to more efficient collection and administration of taxes. The enforcement holes were plugged and taxes collected without discrimination. For example, a large part of the state's gasoline tax, although collected by the state, reverts by law to the local subdivisions. In 1939-1940 the gasoline revenue returned to the local government was over $2,500,-000 more than in the previous biennium.

The improvement in tax administration extended to taxes which provide revenues exclusively for the local subdivisions—such taxes as those on tangible personal property used in business and intangible personal property having a local situs. Rulings of the new state tax commissioner, backed by the new Board of Appeals, were in almost every instance upheld by the state supreme court and were mainly responsible for the increased local revenues. The tax laws were now being put to work and made to function as the legislature had intended when they were written.

In his message to the legislature in 1941, the Governor was able to report that the revenues of local governments from local taxes alone had been increased $11,000,000 in 1940, owing in some measure to the improved administration.

While the state government in Ohio has been moving out of the red in the past four and a half years, into a position from which it can face the future with a substantial backlog of funds ready to be used, an astonishing corollary reduction in local government debts has been going on all over the state. During the four years ending in 1942, the debt of all local governments in Ohio declined from $716,307,126 to $613,110,614, a drop of one-seventh.

This reduction has been general, not merely in the aggregate. Counties reduced their debts more than

$26,250,000, leaving less than $80,000,000 to be paid off; cities paid off $22,350,000; villages reduced their debts one-sixth by paying off $6,327,000; townships have almost completely wiped out theirs; and school districts paid off $48,000,000 of the $175,437,000 they owed in 1938.

If present policies are continued, virtually all the present debts of local governments in Ohio could be liquidated during the 1950's. The state has no debt today, and, in contrast to the $40,000,000 debt in 1938, there is a surplus of about $70,000,000.

The policy of building up a surplus of state funds has been bitterly attacked by the Governor's political opponents; several politically inspired attempts have been made to force a distribution of it among cities and counties. In a speech before the Ohio Society of New York in 1941, Governor Bricker stated the reasons behind his policy.

"When the let-down comes from the now-expanded industrial program, government will need money or people will suffer. Public buildings will be needed and will provide work. Relief demands may enlarge and welfare problems become more serious. I think it is sound government policy to look beyond today and try to build for tomorrow."

The people's approval of their governor's policy was expressed in the 1942 election. The Democratic candidate made a campaign issue of the surplus, and Bricker was re-elected by the largest majority given

142

an Ohio gubernatorial candidate in seventy-nine years. The day after the election, the *Cleveland Plain Dealer* said editorially that the voters had declared "with a great deal of emphasis":

". . . it was no political sin to accumulate a treasury surplus by spending less money than was made available by taxation. What with the added burden of federal taxes that must be assumed for the duration, we in Ohio are fortunate indeed that, in a period of wide governmental extravagance, the state's finances have been maintained on a sound basis."

On the night of his third inauguration day, Governor Bricker went personally before the legislature and recommended removal of the sales tax on food sold in restaurants, hotels, and other public places—also the tax on prescription medicines, thus reducing taxes by approximately $5,000,000 a year.

The Senate responded quickly by passing the repealer, but the House obstinately refused to act. Finally the House Republicans, in caucus, went on record against the repeal.

The Governor did not give up, however. He held a series of conferences with the House leaders and the House Taxation Committee, and he issued several terse public statements pointing out that a tax reduction of $3,000,000 a year was possible, and that he was surprised to find a legislative body which would not make the reduction.

The House leaders answered that they were not

sure enough that the state's revenues from excise taxes would hold up under rationing and other wartime curtailments of business; and besides, they inclined to the theory of Joseph that in the fat years something should be stored away against the lean. In short, they favored getting the money while they could; they would need it later.

The Governor, sorely disappointed, finally issued a statement bowing to the will of the legislative branch, but at the same time having the last word.

"I still believe that this tax on food and medicine should be removed," he declared. "This would spread the benefit to more people than any other tax reduction and consistently exempt all food. In my judgment, a tax reduction would give encouragement to the people. They would know that some public officials are interested in the taxpayers as well as in tax-spenders.

"I made this recommendation in the light of our surplus and estimated revenues. . . . It has not been the practice of preceding General Assemblies of Ohio to appropriate less than estimated revenues, and since relief from taxation seemed most important, we were in a position to afford such tax relief.

"The House of Representatives has not seen fit to effect this tax reduction, expressing the opinion that this money should be saved for postwar needs. Such a decision is clearly within the legislative prerogative. . . . I shall insist that this fund be kept intact for postwar needs, and if there is any attempt to appropriate any part of this money for any other purpose, I shall feel it my duty to veto such appropriations."

The legislature kept the budget within Governor Bricker's estimate, and he was not required to veto any appropriation.

Even with the proposed repeal of the sales taxes on food and medicine, the Governor was able to make the following recommendations in his budget message—recommendations which the legislature carried out:

Aid for the aged to be increased $11,000,000 for the 1943-1944 biennium over the 1941-1942 period.

Assumption by the state of the cost, heretofore borne by the counties, of the care of the feeble-minded in institutions.

Resumption by the state of the payment of the costs of criminal prosecutions in the various counties, an obligation which had not been met for a number of years.

Normal subsidies to local governments to be continued at $12,000,000, plus another $2,000,000 for civilian defense.

Despite the increased yields from some taxes through the wartime industrial boom, the Governor urged continued conservatism in budget-building. He said: "The fiscal policy of conservatism in estimating revenues, plus the practice of keeping expenditure even below conservative appropriations, has made possible our surplus in the general revenue fund."

CHAPTER XI

THE RELIEF "CRISIS"

THE SPOTLIGHT of nationwide publicity swung toward Ohio when Mayor La Guardia of New York, early in December 1939, declared, "People are starving in Cleveland and elsewhere in Ohio." Governor Bricker hastened to reassure the world, "Nobody is starving in the state of Ohio, and nobody will starve in the state of Ohio."

But the story had got into print; press correspondents and cameramen rushed to Cleveland to get the story of the supposed starvation—not, however, until several sensational papers had editorialized with alarm on the situation as they supposed it to be; and weekly news magazines brought out prematurely written articles and spreads of sensationally captioned photographs.

The facts of the relief problem in Ohio and Governor Bricker's handling of it show that not only was there no starvation, but the point at issue was never whether the needy should be cared for; it was simply the question of the division of responsibility among federal, state, and local governments.

In the seven years from 1932 through 1938, the

146

taxpayers of Ohio paid out $137,000,000 for relief—$97,000,000 through the state and $40,000,000 through local governments. On top of that the federal government spent $175,000,000 in Ohio for direct relief in CWA, FERA, and WPA disbursements —which the taxpayers also paid for, of course.

With all this expenditure they bought themselves only an incompetent relief program wastefully and ineptly administered. Succeeding General Assemblies under two governors passed 98 relief bills, all of them stopgaps. Every few months the legislature reassembled, wrestled once more with the hydra-headed problem, and brought forth more temporary relief measures, invariably inadequate in funds, loaded with expedients which next week proved to be inexpedient, and offering little hope of efficiency in administration or economy in handling of the funds provided.

Governor Davey's administration furnished several relief and old-age-pension scandals, and his constant bickering with Washington resulted not only in waste, but in continual uncertainty about the provision for relief and social security. In October 1938 one of these arguments between Columbus and Washington led the federal Social Security Board to withhold from Ohio $1,300,000 in old-age-pension funds on the charge that the Davey administration was using the pension system for the Governor's political purposes. The state had to make up the amount out of its own depleted pocket; and when

Bricker took office the treasury was short just that much which might have been used for unemployment and poor relief.

In his campaign for election Bricker asserted, "It is the job of government to provide adequate relief for all who are in need." People on relief would find their needs "fairly and adequately supplied so long as their need continues," he promised. But at the same time he was determined that the waste of relief funds must stop—that in their concern for the jobless and hungry, the local governments should not go in peril of bankruptcy.

The Davey administration had made ineffectual attempts to divide the cost of relief equally between state and local governments. Bricker adopted the same equal-sharing policy, but with a firm determination to hold local governments to strict account for their half of the bills. When local funds were so largely and so directly involved, he knew, human nature would make the local officials more careful in their spending, thus saving both state and local funds.

Besides contributing half the costs, local government was to have greater responsibility for administering relief. Local officials would have to conform with certain stipulations in the state relief law, and their budgets and expenditures would be checked by the state; but relief workers would be locally employed and responsible to the elected officials of the locality. There would be no state relief workers, no saddling of rural communities with expensive social-worker set-ups, no bureaucrats from Columbus descending upon a city for a few weeks of wrestling and haranguing, falling out with city officials and moving on to a new scene for another round.

Bricker was determined, too, that the state's relief contribution should be included in the regular appropriations bill, a significant move in two ways. In the first place, it recognized for the first time that some measure of poor relief will always be necessary, in good times as well as bad, hence is a permanent responsibility of the state. Second, it implemented Bricker's conviction that the state budget should "clearly disclose and truly reflect" the real overall cost of government, even though the inclusion of the relief item in the appropriations bill would make his budget seem, on superficial observation, to be just so many millions of dollars higher than his predecessors'.

It was no part of Governor Bricker's purpose to be niggardly in the state allowance for relief. During the "recession" year of 1938, when unemployment was at its peak, the state contributed $9,250,000 to local subdivisions for relief, in addition to the proceeds of certain earmarked taxes which would remain levied and distributable for relief in 1939 and 1940. In his budget message to the legislature in 1939, the Governor said:

"In the face of improved business conditions which should reduce the cost of relief, and in the face of unemployment-compensation payments inaugurated the first of this year, provision has been made in the budget for expenditure from the general revenue fund during each year of this biennium in the amount of $9,250,000, being the amount expended in 1938. Estimated revenues for 1939 to be derived from earmarked taxes distributable to the subdivisions for relief, plus the recommended amount from the general revenue fund, show an aggregate recommendation for 1939 for this purpose of $15,160,000, as against an aggregate expenditure by the state for relief in 1938 of $14,222,544."

Pointing to sharp slashes his administration had already made in state operating costs, in the same message he called upon local governments to pare their budgets likewise. This, he said, would provide them with money enough for both the ordinary functions of government and their share of relief costs.

Instead of the $9,250,000 for which he asked, the legislature gave the Governor $10,000,000 for relief, and passed a new relief law providing for distribution of state relief funds on the basis of need rather than according to mathematical formula. Recognizing with the Governor the permanence of the relief problem, the legislature put relief administration in the hands of a cabinet member, the director of public welfare, instead of a state relief director. This change correlated in one department several kinds of aid—poor relief, aid for dependent mothers, for the blind, and for the aged—a plan which made possible a closer check-up on duplications and better all-round administration. Local responsibility was fixed by leaving administration to cities and county relief areas, with local authorities required to get the welfare director's approval of their budgets before receiving their monthly contributions from the state.

The Bricker administration went further in helping local governments to give adequate and efficient relief. When city officials had difficulty in getting the necessary 65 per cent vote on local tax levies for relief purposes, the legislature relaxed a jealously watched safeguard against easy taxation. For the year 1939 it lowered the required vote to a bare majority; then, as notice to cities and counties that economies and restricted local property levies would be insisted upon, it stipulated that in 1940 the required vote would be raised to 55 per cent, and thereafter revert to the original 65 per cent.

As further assistance, the legislature made local-government shares of inheritance and intangible-property taxes available for relief by removing the restrictions on their use and placing them in the general funds of the cities. It also authorized cities to use 10 per cent of their shares of state-collected automobile-license taxes for relief; authorized local subdivisions to issue bonds for as much as 90 per cent—instead of the previously allowed 80 per cent—of their expected shares of the state-collected special relief taxes on public utilities, admissions, beer, malt, and wort; and broadened the powers of local governments to issue bonds.

This relief program met with general approval, but naturally there were some dissenters, among them many city and county officials. In particular, their well-organized high-pressure lobby, the League of Ohio Municipalities, which had unceasingly demanded larger relief appropriations from the state, showed no signs of subsiding. At best, the local officials who made up this lobby in Columbus were skeptical of the adequacy of the program. But it would do for a while, they said; and when things got too bad they could always force a special session of the legislature, show the existence of a "crisis," and get more money. The procedure had worked time and again in the past seven years, and they saw no reason why it should not work again whenever the pinch was felt and they could make the picture look convincing in Columbus.

By late summer, wholesale layoffs by the WPA aggravated the unemployment situation. The state's relief budget had naturally been framed on the presumption that WPA would be continued in the same proportion to unemployment as in 1938. But the WPA rolls were radically slashed in Ohio in the fall of 1939, and by November 1 WPA employment was half what it had been in 1938 on the same date. The federal Social Security Board's own figures showed that more than 55 per cent of the new applicants for relief in Cleveland that fall gave loss of WPA employment as the reason for their distress.

Late in October, Cleveland and Toledo officials asked the Governor to call a special session of the General Assembly to provide more relief money. Cleveland estimated its relief deficit for the year as conservatively $1,425,000.

Special relief levies were generally defeated throughout Ohio in the November elections. Where some levies had formerly been approved by 65 per cent or more of the ballots, they now failed of a bare majority. Mayors of relief-ridden cities clamored that rejection of the levies at the polls was a mandate for distribution of the unappropriated surplus in the state treasury, then between $3,000,000 and $4,000,-000. The Governor, on the contrary, thought it more likely a mandate to brake relief spending. Moreover, he knew that the General Assembly was back of him by an overwhelming majority in every step of his relief program. In fact, a conference with legislative leaders informed him that a majority of the legislature would have tried to enforce a policy considerably more stringent than his.

Mayor Harold H. Burton of Cleveland led a delegation to Columbus to demand more funds. City officials, church leaders, labor leaders, chamber of commerce leaders, Republican politicians—the delegation packed the Governor's office, drawing pictures of the dire results if the state refused them more relief money.

The Governor took the position that the cities had known for over six months that they would get $10,-000,000 from the state for relief that year. The state had kept its share of the bargain largely through economies in operating costs; the cities could not say as much—Cleveland above all, where the city pay roll had been increased. Then he outlined for the delegation five ways in which the city could raise the necessary funds for itself.

The delegation nevertheless went home unappeased and grumbling—even defiant. As the days passed without the calling of a special session, city officials tried to force the issue by applying pressures which had worked in past years. Part of the press in Cleveland, Dayton, and a few other places took up the battle with cries of "A surplus in the state treasury; hunger in Cleveland." The *Dayton Daily News,* James M. Cox's paper, wrote editorially:

"Governor Bricker's stand against a special session to correct the state's neglect makes himself personally responsible for the actual hunger which menaces tens of thousands of his constituents within now a very few days."

Republican newspapers in Dayton were just as insistent in the same vein.

Toward the end of November, Cleveland reduced its food allowance to relief clients and postponed payment of their rents and public utilities bills. The city dropped from its rolls 12,000 cases, all employables and persons with no more than one adult dependent or no minor dependents. At the same time the city took steps to obtain additional federal commodity supplies and tried to stimulate WPA and private employment.

Meantime Governor Bricker was not idle. He was certain that some cities had not made use of all available resources to provide relief funds for themselves. Worse, he knew there were hundreds, perhaps thousands, on relief in Cleveland alone who had no business to be living on public moneys. And, third, he knew that WPA, the stated purpose of which was to keep employable persons off the dole, was not fulfilling its obligation in Ohio. Nevertheless, he proposed that no one should starve there. He would tap all available resources and keep up relief where it was really needed, without asking a reluctant legislature to dip into funds set aside to pay off the state's debt and start the long-overdue welfare-institution building program.

A search of possible sources of relief money turned up a frozen account of $1,800,000 in the state treasury, the excess of revenues from special relief excise taxes above what the various local subdivisions had needed to meet payments on their relief bonds in the past several years. In 1937 the then attorney general had ruled that the money could not be distributed directly for relief. The new attorney general, Thomas J. Herbert, agreed to reopen the question and shortly reversed his predecessor's stand, ruling that the money could be released immediately for relief purposes. A representative of the city of Cleveland was in Columbus when the decision was rendered and went home with a state check for $398,340 in his pocket. Toledo and Dayton likewise received substantial assistance from the distribution.

Department of Taxation records showed another source of funds: Cleveland had for some years had authority to issue tax delinquency bonds in the amount of $1,200,000—"certainly enough," said the Governor, "to tide over its present crisis."

Releasing the bond account in Columbus and the proposed issue of delinquency bonds opened the way for Cleveland to meet fully its deficit in relief bills. City officials demurred, however, expressing doubt of their ability to issue and market the bonds; and Mayor Burton held out for a special session.

On November 28, several hundred "relief clients" marched on Cleveland City Hall. The *Cleveland News* said next day:

"The crowd was rounded up by the Workers' Alliance—and by the brand-new 'Association of Unemployed on Direct and Work Relief.' The Alliance is a stooge for the Communist party, and the Association is headed by C. B. Cowan, who is regarded by Stalin Communists as a Trotsky Communist. . . . Don't be fooled by the noise."

On November 29 Governor Bricker made a final refusal to call a special session of the legislature. The *Cleveland News* feared the Governor did not have "the conception of the want that exists here," but recalled:

"He did warn the cities then [spring of 1939] that $10,000,000 a year would be all the state could and would contribute. He has enforced his notable state operating economies without favor. Many will feel that he has the right to expect the same economizing in connection with the state's relief help."

Even then the Governor did not slacken in his efforts to help Cleveland. On December 4 the state advanced the city $192,000 to pay for the care of insane and feeble-minded patients in city and private hospitals there. Although this money was later returned to the state, according to stipulation, its advancement supplied $192,000 to the city's general revenue fund at a time when it was needed to pay relief bills.

To help restore the WPA program, the Governor sent the state Highway Department's maintenance engineer to Cleveland to work out additional highway projects so as to open up 3,000 additional WPA jobs for federal participation; and similar WPA-state highway projects were developed in the Toledo area.

Having taken these steps to tide the cities over the emergency, Governor Bricker thought the time had come to "speak plainly about the relief situation in Ohio." In a formal statement he declared:

"No one will argue but that the hungry must be fed. The question at issue is whether or not the cities are shirking their own responsibility in failing to use present resources to meet the problems.

"The cost of relief has been running into millions of dollars annually for a number of years. We must pare down large-scale relief until we can be sure that only those who are actually in need are on the relief rolls, and that all local governments are doing everything within their power to help themselves.

"Local needs must be taken care of at home to a greater and greater extent. It is easy for city officials to run to Columbus or to Washington to ask for more money, and then sit on their hands and issue statements to the newspapers until they get it."

The state had cut pay rolls more than $3,000,000 in the first nine months of 1939, the Governor went on; but the pay rolls of the city of Cleveland had risen steadily, year by year, until the 1938 pay roll was $1,400,000 higher than the 1936, and another $300,000 boost was indicated for 1939.

"The state has met its financial difficulties by practicing economy," he said. "Is it asking too much to expect county and city governments who are asking for more money from the state for relief, to do likewise?"

At least part of Cleveland's difficulty, the Governor charged, arose from "political manipulation of the WPA. In November of 1938, an election year, there were 74,167 on the WPA rolls in Cuyahoga County. Since the election, the number has dropped to as low as 29,125. WPA jobs should be available for people who need them, not for mere political workers."

The state had recently called the attention of Cleveland city officials to the city's obligation to reregister relief clients; and 23 per cent of those previously on relief had not applied for continued aid when the reregistration was held. "There is no way of telling," observed the Governor, "how long those who were not eligible for relief had been on the rolls."

A check-up on relief clients at about the same time revealed that more than 2,000 recipients of public aid in Cleveland had been driving automobiles. Where were they driving to? Certainly not to work, for they were presumably either unemployed or unemployable. Where did they get money for gasoline?

The Cleveland relief commissioner ordered relief clients to turn in their auto license tags if they expected to stay on relief. Two hundred and thirty-two tags were turned in; 100 relief clients specifically refused to turn theirs in, and their relief was cut off; some of the remainder were among those who failed to reregister for relief.

The day after Governor Bricker issued his statement exposing the relief situation in Cleveland, the state Board of Tax Appeals issued a formal holding that Cleveland had authority to issue and sell up to $1,200,000 of the bonds the Governor had suggested. Mayor Burton immediately announced that the bonds would be issued and said that "a calamity has been avoided. There is no one starving in Cleveland, and there will be no starving at least between now and some time in January." The financial relief obtained through the state's co-operation, distribution of surplus commodities, and an anticipated restoration of 6,000 workers to the WPA rolls, would, he said, "ease the situation to some extent." Besides, he observed, "the employment situation is rapidly getting better in Cleveland."

According to the Mayor's own statement, the city was able "to restore its relief operations to the regular basis needed to take care of essential cases."

The financial crisis in Cleveland was over; but the tale of "starvation" was abroad through the nation. Visioning street riots, a road show actually canceled its Cleveland dates. The story was even publicized in Germany—as a sign of democratic decadence. It was another three weeks before the tumult subsided.

Mayor La Guardia's connections with the Roosevelt administration gave weight to his words; he was presumed to have his information straight from official sources. Even the more conservative press was inclined to give credence to the statement of so prominent a public figure as the mayor of New York city. The Mayor, for his part, was entertaining hopes for the future of his American Labor party.

Secretary of the Interior Harold L. Ickes joined the pack with some acid comment; on December 8, after Bricker's plan had already averted the crisis,

President Roosevelt himself charged that Ohio was not meeting its state obligations.

Governor Bricker promptly pointed out in reply that in his administration "nearly every state department is being operated at a lower cost than last year. When the federal authorities are able to say the same about the cost of operating the federal agencies, I shall be more willing to accept their advice as to how to run our state."

With Mayor La Guardia, Secretary Ickes, and the President himself in the cast, the sensational drama attracted other actors. David Lasser, head of the Workers' Alliance, announced that he would go to Ohio and "insist on action." The Associated Press quoted him from Washington as threatening a "protest march" on the state capitol. Governor Bricker charged the President with letting Lasser use the White House as a "sounding board for communistic and revolutionary propaganda." The protest march never materialized.

John Owens, president of the United Mine Workers of the Ohio district, at that time an affiliate of the CIO, asked the President to send army soup kitchens into Ohio, and the President said he would. Governor Bricker retorted, "If soup kitchens are put in Cleveland or elsewhere in Ohio, it will be purely for New Deal political effect." Not a soup kitchen was ever dispatched to Ohio.

Excited radio commentators issued regular bulletins to a waiting world, as if at any moment they

161

might be reading out a casualty list. Editor Raymond Moley later observed:

"To hear supposedly impartial commentators tell of that battle, when it was at its height, you would have thought of Bricker as a kind of Silas Marner, gleefully fondling the state money while the hungry people of Ohio were dropping like flies."

Not all the newspaper and radio men pitched headlong into sensationalism. There were some who saw and reported the truth. They saw plenty of distress— such distress as they might have found at the very moment in New York city or in scores of others throughout the United States. But as for starvation— there was none.

James L. Killgallen, of the International News Service, whose byline is authoritative around the world, looked into the situation in Ohio from all angles and reported:

"A striking fact in the relief situation in the various cities was the attitude of the reliefers themselves. There have been no disturbances. There has been a disposition to have faith in civic leaders in the belief that they were doing all they could to raise funds and to see that no one would go hungry. There has not been any starvation."

Warren Moscow, able Albany correspondent of the *New York Times,* was another who found no starvation. Fulton Lewis, the Mutual Broadcasting System's keen reporter, made an on-the-spot check-up in Cleveland and other Ohio cities, and then reported on his coast-to-coast network:

"There is discomfort, but it doesn't reach the point of dire distress. There is neither starvation nor a crisis."

Like many a newspaper reporter, editorial writer, columnist, and observer, Lewis sensed that national attention was focused on the dispute because in some quarters the Governor was looked upon as a dark-horse candidate for president in 1940. Philip W. Porter, one of Ohio's most respected newspapermen, put it this way in his column in the *Cleveland Plain Dealer*:

"When Bricker seemed to show more interest in a state surplus than in feeding clients in Cleveland and was in controversy with a fellow Republican, the New Deal crowd saw an opportunity to pin a label on Bricker. . . . It is always fair game to knock off a potential rival in the Republican camp."

Porter went on to express the belief that the Ohio incident had been seized upon by the New Dealers "for propaganda purposes."

While the sensational publicity was at its height, Governor Bricker, in full confidence that he had taken adequate steps to provide for necessary relief, went to New York city to deliver an address. He was in fighting trim when he rose before the Ohio Society of New York and in hearing of a national radio audience slugged back at his critics.

He began by asserting that Ohio had "not been

163

taken over by the White House or the Department of the Interior. The people of America must awaken to a realization of how far this federal administration will go in its attempt to smear the good name of a state or an administration which dares to do a good job financially as well as in social service."

He outlined the provisions Ohio had made to aid local governments, particularly in unemployment and poor relief—provisions more generous in amount and more pliable to varying local situations than in the preceding years. Then he turned to the role of the federal government in relief:

"During the past year, WPA employment in Ohio has been cut by Washington 53.6 per cent, while the average reduction for the whole United States for the same period was only 43.9 per cent. That discrepancy is not justified by any consideration of relief needs. That picture would indicate that Ohio is being punished. Why? Is it because Ohio voted Republican last year? . . .

"The issue is clear-cut: Shall relief, including work relief, WPA, or whatever it may be called, be administered honestly, fairly, with due regard to the needs of the people, or shall it be administered as a political racket—padding the WPA rolls in election years and forgetting the needs in non-election years, carrying the burden so that the federal government can take credit when a national election is on, and passing the buck back to the states and local communities in the other years? This is a question which

164

the American people must answer; and in it is involved a fundamental question of public morals. . . .

"There have been attacks made on Ohio and on me personally. Most New Dealers have contempt for any government authority or public official who does balance a budget, who does administer relief honestly, who does save public money, or who shows any interest whatever in the taxpayer. No, it is the political discrimination of the national administration against Ohio—obviously for the purpose of discrediting a state administration—that has caused the trouble. . . .

"I do not propose to be clubbed into a position of fear or silence in the conduct of affairs in the state of Ohio when the very foundations of public morality, political decency, simple honesty, and fundamental human integrity have been eaten away by the unblushing political immorality of the New Deal in its relations to human needs and relief. . . .

"It is not in my heart to flinch before a public crack-down from the White House simply because I have refused steadfastly to permit the administration of public assistance in the state of Ohio to become the football of disgraceful partisan politics in Washington, New York, and the Department of the Interior. . . .

"As governor of Ohio, I have made it my business to know the relief situation throughout the state. We have been meeting and will continue to meet our

165

relief responsibilities in an honest, straightforward fashion.

"I have also an interest in the relief of overburdened taxpayers, in the farmer who works from sunup until sundown, and who often receives too small a part of the nation's income. I have an interest in the homeowner who is now burdened with heavy taxes. I have an interest in the relief of the man who has a job, but who for every four days' work done gives one to the government in taxes. . . .

"I do not seek the approbation of those office holders who revel in their accomplishments as financial hitch-hikers. But I do seek the honest, man-to-man respect of the great body of our citizenry who are striving earnestly to restore this country to the pay-as-you-go program of solid American prosperity.

"I do seek the co-operation of those groups who are endeavoring in the spirit of sincerity, patience, and good will to work out a lasting solution of our social and economic problems. The people of this mighty nation can solve those problems. . . .

"The political pork barrel never can become the wheel of American progress."

On the same day that Governor Bricker delivered his address in New York city, Mayor Burton of Cleveland was writing the Governor a letter. It was on the Governor's desk when he returned from his trip.

The mayor said he was writing because of "the large amount of misinformation which has been

publicized about the relief emergency in Cleveland."
He summarized the situation at length, and the first
statement under his Number One heading was:
"There has been no starvation in Cleveland."

"While this experience caused hardship, it cannot properly be described as a condition of starvation," he wrote. "There was at no time indicated by
the state government any disregard of the seriousness
of the need nor any desire not to meet that need. On
the other hand, the state found ways to take new
steps and to grant new authority to the city of Cleveland which made it possible to relieve the situation
and immediately upon such authority being made
available, this city, in full co-operation with the state,
made use of those means."

By the simple expedient of summoning the General
Assembly into special session and dumping the problem in their laps, Governor Bricker might have side-
stepped the whole relief controversy and the storm
of criticism it engendered. But to him this very controversy was a test of the whole fabric of American
government and sound political economy; he pre-
ferred to meet the issue head-on, solve the problem
with means already available, if that were possible,
and afterwards face fearlessly the criticism directed
at himself.

By February of 1940, animosities of a few weeks
earlier had cooled, and representatives of the various
cities, the Governor, and WPA were sitting down

together to work out an effective relief program. State and local welfare heads compared notes regularly thereafter, and there was very nearly complete understanding on all phases of the problem which had so long plagued the state.

When the June relief budgets of the cities showed that the state appropriation was not large enough to see them through the rest of the year, the Governor, feeling that the various defects in local financing had been remedied and the available local resources were being used as fully as possible, asked the General Assembly, in special session, to make additional state funds available for relief. The legislature granted out of old, unexpended, and unobligated relief funds an outright subsidy of $1,460,388 and a loan of $333,333 to local relief areas.

In the 1940 campaign, the Democratic candidate for governor naturally raised Bricker's handling of the relief problem as an issue. The response of the voters was to re-elect Bricker by a majority of 364,-467 votes and a percentage larger than any in the past 77 years. He carried 77 out of 88 counties, including Cuyahoga (Cleveland), Lucas (Toledo), and Montgomery (Dayton), the three areas which had presented him with the biggest relief problems the year before. Cuyahoga County gave him a majority of 51,000 as compared with his loss of that county two years earlier by 64,000 votes. At the same time Mayor Burton, the Republican nominee for United States senator, lost his own county by 900 votes, although he carried the state, running 220,000 votes behind Bricker.

During the months leading up to and early in his campaign for re-election, Bricker was more widely mentioned for the presidential nomination than before. Another prominent possibility in 1940 was Ohio's junior senator, Robert A. Taft, son of President and Chief Justice William Howard Taft. As an ex-state senator and able son of a distinguished father, "Bob" Taft had gone to the 1936 convention as Ohio's favorite son. In 1939, as a United States senator, fresh from his triumph at the polls in a resurgent Republican state, he was more logically a standard-bearer from Ohio than in 1936—and he earnestly desired the nomination for President.

For a while, it looked as if Ohio might have two favorite sons in 1940, but in July 1939 Bricker gave Taft the go-ahead signal. "Any assumption that I have been a candidate for President or have been working at it in any sense is not true," Governor Bricker said.

Still, the Bricker talk continued. In November 1939, the governor was compelled to disown a political headquarters which was about to be opened in Chicago in his name. "I haven't sanctioned it and I won't sanction anything of the kind," he declared. As late as April 1940, an unauthorized "Draft Bricker Committee" was formed in New York city and an unsanctioned "Bricker-for-President Association" was started in Illinois.

In May Bricker was elected a delegate-at-large to the national convention, pledged to Taft, and at Philadelphia he was named chairman of the Ohio delegation, which was to place Taft's name in nomination. Bricker was widely looked upon as a "dark horse" possibility should a deadlock develop among Taft, Thomas E. Dewey of New York, and Wendell L. Willkie of Indiana. At a press conference on the eve of the convention, a newspaper man asked Bricker who Ohio's "second choice" would be.

"We are going to vote for Taft until he is nominated," Bricker replied.

When Willkie won out over Taft, Bricker, as chairman of the Ohio delegation and with Taft's sanction, obtained recognition of the convention chairman and moved that the nomination be made unanimous. He campaigned for Willkie that fall, not only in Ohio but in neighboring states, in the midst of his own campaign for re-election as governor.

Asked recently if there had been a Taft-Bricker agreement in 1940 by which the Governor was to support Senator Taft for the presidential nomination that year and the Senator was to support Bricker in 1944, as has been persistently reported, the Governor replied:

"There was no semblance of any agreement. Nor has there ever been any semblance of any agreement on any appointment of any kind or character as to what I would do or as to what the other fellow would do."

170

CHAPTER XII

WAR AND DEFENSE

A COLUMBUS citizen driving to work on the morning of January 13, 1941, may have glanced into a small gray coupé drawn up beside him at a traffic light. If he did, he received a neighborly smile from beneath the neatly turned gray hatbrim of the big man jackknifed over the wheel, and recognized the Governor driving himself to his second inauguration. Liveried chauffeurs, motorcycle escorts, blaring sirens have as little place as possible in Governor Bricker's life. Anecdotes illustrating his simple, homely way of living are no novelty to Ohioans; but the citizens of Lebanon, eighty miles from the capital, have a particular one which they never stop telling.

Shortly after he became governor, Bricker arranged to attend the unveiling in Lebanon of a historical plaque on the Golden Lamb, oldest hotel in operation in Ohio, which had entertained such distinguished guests as Charles Dickens, Henry Clay, and John Quincy Adams in the days of the stagecoach. The villagers stood before the plaque, craning down the road for a sight of the official arrival, prick-

171

ing their ears for the first sound of the sirens. The road remained empty of official cars, and the crowd was getting restless when a small stir on the fringes grew into a breathless cheering as the Governor and Mrs. Bricker picked their way down the street from their small car parked a block away. It seemed to them the natural way to arrive; and the Lebanonites are still telling how much they liked it.

At the second inaguration there was no booming cannon in the statehouse yard, no bands or confetti or out-of-doors platforms. Ohio's artillery pieces, like the 12,000 officers and men of her National Guard, were in training for national defense. The Governor took the oath of office in the capitol rotunda, with a small audience tiered on the four double staircases rising from the circular hall.

As he stood encircled by glass cases containing Ohio's battle flags of four wars, the Governor's thoughts dwelt upon the possibility of war for the United States and its implications for the people under his care. The first draftees had already left the state under the Selective Service Act of 1940, and the nation was drawing closer to war each day. In his inaugural address the Governor said:

"Two great philosophies of government and opposing forces in society are in a death struggle. The answer to this conflict may determine the character of society for centuries yet to be. Shall man govern himself? Shall he have a voice in the conduct of his own life and a vote in the destiny of his government,

The Brickers Today at the
Governor's Mansion

or shall his daily existence be completely subservient to a political autocracy? The conflict is age-old, but waged with an intensity today more than ever before experienced.

"America is on the side of liberty, freedom, progress, hope, and individual opportunity. In our society, in this representative government, the individual's place is emphasized. For him, our government exists. For his greater opportunity all public servants should strive.

"During the next two years, the outcome of that conflict which has brought nations to war may be determined more and more by the action of America and by the spirit of our people in devotion to the preservation of our ideals written into our constitutional form of government."

Referring to the problems facing his own new administration, the Governor admonished the local governments to save money wherever possible so that the necessary taxes for defense would not place too great a burden on the people.

"I know of no better way that Ohio might assume her responsibility in this defense program than in doing a good job in local government," he said.

In conclusion the Governor pleaded for the concerted effort of every citizen in the defense program.

"Seeing the destruction that is rampant in the world, we ought to have a new devotion to our country and our kind of government. I call upon every citizen of the state to give not alone of his money to

173

his government, but of his time and ability. Our soldiers serve on meager pay in camp. Let their sacrifice be met by an equal unselfish devotion to duty at home. Industry must respond, and labor must accept its responsibility. I plead for a new appreciation of the spiritual values which we can have by preserving America free and undefiled. In this dark hour in the world's history, I plead particularly for a new appreciation of the American way of life and living."

Intelligent long-range planning by the Bricker administration enabled Ohio to slip smoothly into wartime gear with a minimum of strain and confusion. Several months before January 1941 the Governor had appointed a committee to co-ordinate industrial activities with national defense. The committee sought out and publicized the availability, sometimes in unexpected or out-of-the-way places, of vital tools and machine parts, and the shops, many of them small, which could produce them. Also, a survey was made of industrial and natural resources which were tapped later in the augmented war effort.

Going before the legislature early in 1941, the Governor asked it to: establish a state council of defense and authorize the appointment of district and local councils; increase the state highway patrol from 200 to 300 men; and establish a state guard to defend the commonwealth in the absence of the Ohio National Guard.

174

The legislature complied, and the state's defenses were put into such good condition that no special session of the General Assembly was necessary at any time during 1941 and 1942 to enact special wartime laws—this despite the fact that the legislature adjourned in May, seven months before Pearl Harbor.

Early in June 1941, two months before the state Defense Council could be officially established under the new law, the Governor appointed an unofficial council. By the time the law became effective, this council was organized and already had many operations under way, and others mapped out, ready to function.

The newly created Ohio State Guard was organized and in training camp by mid-August 1941, and a state naval militia was also established.

Nearly two years before Pearl Harbor, the state Bureau of Aeronautics, directed by Earle L. Johnson, with the assistance of the federal government, started civilian aviation training at several Ohio colleges and other points. When war came, 4,500 students had obtained certificates as civilian fliers from these training courses. Upon the foundation of that training, the Army was able to turn out hundreds of military fliers in a relatively short time.

Within a few weeks after war was declared, Director Johnson was made national commander of the Civilian Air Patrol, with the rank of lieutenant colonel, a post which he has filled with eminent success

175

in the war against submarines and in other patrol duties.

In 1940, before its federalization, the State Employment Office made an intensive study of manpower needed to operate Ohio industry at peak. This was perhaps the first—certainly one of the first—surveys of its kind in the nation, and it became the pattern for reports from every state to the Office of Production Management.

On the day the Japanese attacked Pearl Harbor, Ohio had 276 local defense councils besides the state council, all of them functioning. The Governor had himself appointed the local councils upon recommendations of local authorities. When the news of war came, the Governor lay in University Hospital in Columbus, his right leg in a cast reaching above the knee. He had just had an operation to repair the tendons in the leg which had been injured in a badminton game several weeks earlier. From his bed he ordered the mobilization of the state's defense forces and telegraphed Ohio's support to President Roosevelt.

With her machinery organized and functioning, Ohio swung quickly and easily into the various phases of the war effort. Her program for salvaging vital materials functioned smoothly under Lee J. Pierson, who for two years had been acting as state supervisor of salvage in the Bricker program of conservation of materials.

"Washington is well pleased with the Ohio defense

job. I want to congratulate Governor Bricker." So a representative of OPA declared when the state Council of Defense launched its program for putting rubber restrictions into effect. The state Defense Council also administered the earliest phases of the rationing program, and several council officials were transferred to OPA when that agency took over the program.

Besides conducting blackout and dimout drills, the state Defense Council established a state control center and alerting system, in conjunction with the Fire Marshal's Division conducted defense training schools, and arranged for exchanging fire-fighting equipment throughout the state.

In time the number of local defense councils reached 925, with over 600,000 enrolled volunteers, of whom half were trained for defense in case of sabotage, air-raids, or other disaster; over 200,000 were trained for civilian-service duties. Thirty-seven out of every thousand people in Ohio are prepared to perform defense and service duties on the home front.

At the Governor's request, the state Board of Control made $2,000,000 available to local governments for financing local defense in 1942—money provided out of funds appropriated for unemployment relief and no longer needed for that purpose. In 1943 he asked the legislature for a similar amount for distribution to local governments for civilian defense in that year and in 1944; but, after seeing some of the expenditures local subdivisions had made in the name of civilian defense in 1942, the legislature reduced the amount to $1,250,000.

The Highway Department took a large share of the increased responsibilities of wartime. The construction of military access roads and highways serving factories engaged in war production were given priority. To help in moving military equipment and personnel, the department's engineers rated for army traffic the 25,000 bridges in the state of over 20-foot span.

A War Transportation Committee was set up under the Highway Department to plan the staggering of working hours, share-the-ride programs, and programs for efficient automobile operation. Some 2,400 share-the-ride depots were established throughout the state, and 1,800 victory-speed signs (35 miles per hour) were erected on the state's highway system, making Ohio the first state to put up this kind of sign.

The Highway Department organized its own emergency disaster unit, training 6,000 men and keeping every kind of vehicle ready for service. Special crews were trained for highway clearance, demolition, bridge repair, traffic control, and so on. Complete evacuation plans were drawn, even to housing, hospitalization, and feeding. A central message center was set up for control and co-ordination of the defense system, and was given a practical test under real emergency conditions during the Ohio

River flood of December 1942. In that emergency the Highway Department's disaster units moved into threatened areas ahead of the flood and removed 3,000 families to safety. Not a single life was lost in the flood as a result, a record never before matched when the Ohio River has flooded.

The augmented state highway patrol, under Colonel Lynn J. Black, its superintendent, trained 3,500 members of the American Legion for auxiliary police duty; trained war-plant guards and guarded war-plant strategic transportation areas; co-operated with the FBI, military Intelligence officers, and local police departments in preventing sabotage and in making investigations; convoyed troops; and made an extensive survey of every critical war plant, power system, communication system, airport, railroad center, and vital utility in the state.

The Public Utilities Commission established a program of co-operation among all common carriers to speed up transportation of war supplies and personnel. The commission required all carriers to file with it information about the capacity, efficiency, and availability of equipment, thus enabling it to serve as a clearing-house for emergency action.

Early in the war, Ohio constructed a new warehouse and garage at Camp Perry, formerly a training ground for the Ohio National Guard, and in 1942 turned all the facilities of the huge camp over to the Army for an induction center, training camp, and ordnance proving ground.

The state Department of Taxation altered the basis of taxation on gasoline brought into the state, making it possible to divert 8,000 to 10,000 railway tank cars to the eastern seaboard—cars previously used for the monthly distribution of liquid fuel in Ohio and upon the contents of which the tax actually was levied.

The Department of Public Welfare gave special attention to the need for daytime care of children whose mothers are employed in defense industries. The Department of Health has tested the blood specimens of every draft registrant examined by the 330 selective service boards in the state. The department's Bureau of Vital Statistics went on a day-and-night basis to provide over 100,000 birth certificates for defense workers.

The Department of Education established farm-machine repair classes for both children and adults to help conserve farm machinery, and started schools for training city boys and girls for farm work during periods of labor shortage. Co-operative courses in which high-school students work half-time in industries and receive half-time technical courses in school are another contribution from this department.

Under a vocational training program reaching into 93 communities, 300,000 workers were trained for war-production jobs between July 1940 and April 1943.

In the spring of 1943, when the labor and machinery shortage, plus long-continued rains, set the farmers back in their plowing and planting schedules and threatened the production of essential crops, particularly corn and soy beans, the state Highway Department put 200 state-owned tractors and several hundred laborers at the disposal of the farmers. In two weeks these tractors and men had plowed, disked, and dragged 10,000 acres of land which would otherwise have lain idle. Meanwhile the highway workers carried on their own duties for the state by staggering the highway work to let the men work in the fields in shifts.

In the fall of the same year highway trucks and workers were put at the disposal of the canning industry so that Ohio, which ranks fourth among the states in the commercial canning of vegetables, could make its full contribution to the world's food supply.

In both instances the workers were paid by the farmers and canneries for the time they worked for them; and the fuel likewise was provided out of private funds.

The state of Ohio has invested liberally in federal government securities as a contribution to the war effort. Treasurer of State Don H. Ebright announced on October 1, 1943, that $126,109,300 had been invested in federal bonds out of the state's various trust funds, and $35,000,000 out of the general revenue fund, making a total of $161,109,300.

Meanwhile, the attention of the Governor and his administration turned to planning for the postwar period. The Highway and Public Welfare departments have drawn up detailed blueprints for postwar construction projects, many of which already have been approved for co-operation of the federal government. The 1943 legislature authorized the Governor to appoint a postwar planning commission to prime the wheels of government for the problems which the peace will bring.

Governor Bricker's third inauguration, in January of 1943, reflected, in its simplicity and earnest undertones, his consciousness of graver responsibilities, of the people's need for wiser guidance than ever before. Wearing a blue business suit, he stood before a cluster of the flags of the United Nations in a corner of the reception room outside his office. During the administration of the oath, his son held the 150-year-old family Bible, open at the Governor's choice to Proverbs 3:1—"My son, forget not my law, but let thine heart keep my commandments."

CHAPTER XIII

FEDERAL ENCROACHMENT

ONE OF THE gravest threats to self-government, in Governor Bricker's opinion, lies in the failure of some local and state governments to resist the trend toward centralization of control. He hates the principle of centralization in the abstract; and in the particular he hates the voraciousness of the federal government in gathering controls in Washington during recent years. But equally repugnant to him is the supineness of occasional local governments in surrendering their prerogatives and responsibilities to absentee administrators; by their failure to resist the trend, they run the risk of losing the struggle by default. In his first inaugural address he made it clear that he would oppose federal encroachment in all its forms.

"We bow to the exercise of the paramount power of the federal government within its proper sphere. But representative government must be founded upon the interests of the local communities, and the sovereignty of the states is but an expression of that local interest. We shall oppose, with all the ability we possess, the abuse of federal power, when it means the destruction of local self-government within its proper sphere. That is the foundation of our representative system. That was a fundamental demand of the American electorate in the recent election. Our response shall be in making state government meet the needs of the people.

"There must be a revitalization of state and local government throughout the nation. The individual citizen must again be conscious of his responsibilities to his government, and alert to the preservation of his rights as a citizen under it. That cannot be done by taking government further away, but by keeping it at home."

Throughout his administration this has been the note most insistently sounded—the necessity of keeping government close to the people by maintaining a separation of powers between federal and state, state and local governments, each to be responsible in its own sphere.

In this respect Governor Bricker has been more than the governor of Ohio—he has been the leader, as well as the reflector, of the political thinking of her people. He has never once let the issue lie; he has opposed encroachment in action and in words wherever it has appeared. His battle with the federal government and the city of Cleveland over the handling of unemployment relief was based on his belief that federal, state, and local government must each do its share to meet the obligation of financing relief measures; but administrative responsibility must be as largely as possible in local hands.

He has championed resistance to centralization in many forums. Keynoting the Republican state convention in Indiana in May 1940, he urged his party to "demand the decentralization of government." In December of the same year, in an address before the Investment Bankers' Association of America at Hollywood, Florida, he flayed the centralization of authority in Washington, declaring: "The best way to stop encroachment is to do a good job back home, prove the vitality and necessity of state government." In October 1941 he told the Ohio Society of New York:

"The federal government cannot encompass the whole field. It should not try. . . . The states are the laboratories of governmental processes. They learn from each other. The federal government has learned and can learn much from the states' experience. The states today are the real expression of local self-government. They reflect local interest. . . . Our states, preserved, are the surest defense against dictatorship."

In his message to the Ohio Legislature in January 1943, he said:

"There are those in government today, greedy for power, who would destroy state and local government. They have set up boards, bureaus, and commissions with arbitrary authority to dominate our daily lives . . . There is abroad today the desire for centralizing power and socializing government which knows no limits and seeks to become master of all. We can here [in the state legislature] prove to the world that local government is more than a name, and that it is a living force among free men and women."

The Governor is in no sense a traditionalist when he takes this view. He realizes that changing conditions—such changes as the improvement in transportation and communication facilities has made in the world of today—from time to time make necessary a reappraisal and reapportionment of the functions of government among the federal, state, and local spheres. But in his opinion there is never a time when it is necessary to re-place the processes of government as specifically divided by the Constitution among the legislative, executive, and judicial branches. He is as vigorously opposed to bureaucracy as to unnecessary centralization.

In 1943 he said to the legislature: "The autocracy of bureaucracy is as reprehensible as autocracy under any other guise."

Several months earlier he had declared in New York: "We are fighting autocracy and lust for power throughout the world; let's beat it down at home."

Still earlier he had warned: "Too many are in office who have an insatiable desire to meddle in other people's business."

Inevitably, the Governor's attitude toward centralization and bureaucracy have brought him to sharp clashes with the Roosevelt administration, some of them veritable slugging matches; and Bricker has never pulled his punches. One of the hottest and most typical is his fight against the federal government's attempt to absorb the unemployment-compensation systems of the states in 1941 and 1942. The Governor and Herschel Atkinson, administrator of the Ohio Bureau of Unemployment Compensation, took a leading part in defending the states' right to control their own systems.

When he originally advocated unemployment insurance in 1934, President Roosevelt insisted that the states were the most logical units for administration of unemployment-compensation benefits. He proposed, however, that these systems be included in a general framework of federal social-security legislation, and that the federal government control and invest the reserve funds of the state systems. His proposals were incorporated in the federal Social Security Act of 1935, and in 1936 the Ohio legislature enacted a compensation law which conformed with the federal act.

The reorganization of the Unemployment Compensation Commission into the Bureau of Unemployment Compensation, together with the efficient guidance of Atkinson, soon put Ohio high among all states in administration of unemployment compensation. In 1939 Ohio paid out more than any other state in benefits per individual claimant, an average of $106.82. That same year she ranked second lowest among all states in cost of operating the unemploy-ment-compensation system.

And while she was receiving commendation from the Social Security Board in Washington for the most efficient job of all states in economical administration of unemployment compensation, Ohio was hanging up a notable record in the State Employment Service, which was operated in conjunction with the Bureau of Unemployment Compensation and under the same administrator.

Ohio had founded the first state employment service in the United States, in 1890. It had served the workers of the state admirably in recurrent periods of unemployment; and when job placements throughout the United States began to rise in 1939, Ohio's increase in placements was 64 per cent as compared with a national average of 29 per cent. In 1940 the Employment Service found jobs for 184,-000 men and women; in 1941 the number was over 200,000.

When the United States Civil Service Commission was confronted with the task of securing personnel for defense plants in Ohio in 1939 and 1940, it was understaffed and untrained. The State Employment Service stepped into the gap and did the job. At a social-security meeting in Cleveland, one of the ranking officers of the United States Civil Service Commission declared:

"I do not know what our offices would have done if it had not been for the Ohio State Employment

Service. It took the load for us and produced outstanding results."

The Supplies Priority and Allocation Board, established in the fall of 1941 by President Roosevelt, asked the Ohio State Employment Service for a survey of the state's basic industrial labor supply and production and the effect of priorities in Ohio, allowing ninety days for compiling the survey. In ten days the completed survey was in Washington. On October 8, 1941, Administrator Atkinson received a telegram from the chief of the priorities branch, labor division, of the Supplies Priority and Allocation Board: "Let me congratulate you on first class job of surveys of effect of priorities on Ohio communities."

Here, then, was an example of a state government, through one of its departments, functioning efficiently in a time of pressure to give full support to the federal government as it faced the increasing needs of the country's defense. Ohio was living up to its governor's precept: "The best way to stop encroachment is to do a good job back home, prove the vitality and necessity of state government." It was proving that "local government is more than a name and that it is a living force, . . . the strong foundation of the federal system."

Meanwhile, the amended unemployment-compensation law had been passed, and by late summer of 1941 was in effect. Robert Goodwin, a federal coordinator, said of it the day it became effective:

189

"It is in reality a broad interpretation of human rights. It conforms more nearly with the basic concept of unemployment compensation as expressed in the present federal law. Because it has been liberalized to extend the benefits to the worker, it is now an even stronger link in the chain of social security."

Yet all the while these words of praise were coming from Washington, the Bureau of Unemployment Compensation and the State Employment Service in Ohio were constantly harassed by the same Washington. Two investigations of the department were made by federal probers in two years' time. At one time fourteen investigators together pored over the books of the bureau, and every personnel transaction was investigated, considerably interfering with the work of the bureau. Nothing came of either inquiry.

Then, late in the summer of 1941, Governor Bricker was informed that federal investigators were calling upon employees discharged by the bureau, trying to get affidavits of Hatch Act violations by the Bricker administration. Finally the investigators came to the Governor and asked for rooms in the department where they could question all the employees about political activities which might come under the Hatch Act. This was the day, said the Governor, when Democratic leaders in Columbus were summoning federal employees to a certain hotel room to solicit them for contributions. "If you want to go into campaign contributions, all right," he told them.

190

"Let's go into it." His voice could be heard in the corridor through two solid doors.

At that, the investigators decided they did not need rooms after all, and the federal Civil Service Commission dropped the inquiry.

Governor Bricker afterward characterized the inquiry as a "fishing expedition" and a "political raid." He told the story in detail before the Ohio Society of New York:

"Claims were made of complaints, and that affidavits of alleged violations were in their possession. I asked for the charges and affidavits. They were refused. I advised them that if there were any violations of law, a hearing would be necessary—that I would take care of the violations myself.

"Then I was shown three of a claimed fifty affidavits. They consisted of the most trivial and insignificant matters, no violations of laws, signed by discharged employees. One involved campaign stickers on automobiles. They happened to favor my candidacy for re-election in 1940. I asked for the remainder and was refused. The reason given was that our attorney general would get counter-affidavits. It then was apparent that they did not want the truth, but were trying to put on a 'smear' campaign to 'get' someone.

"Then, on October 4, the truth was revealed and the purpose of the investigation became apparent. The President was to ask Congress to federalize all of these 51 state and territorial departments. An attack of some kind on Ohio was necessary—maybe to get some votes in Congress from Ohio. Maybe the state administration had to be discredited in the public mind.

"The Ohio record was good, so the Hatch Act and Civil Service were to be used in Ohio. As long as I am governor of Ohio, I will fight such a move. I will fight to protect the fund of $206,000,000 in the un-employment-compensation fund to Ohio's credit for Ohio labor and employees. I will fight to protect the progressive law we now have. I will fight to preserve our merit rating and our own industrial interests.

"More important than all this—I will fight to maintain local government in Ohio. We elected state officials are responsible to the people of our state. If we do not know more about the needs and inter-ests and hopes of the citizens of our states than all the co-ordinators, attorney examiners, investigators, and bureaucratic order-takers and -givers that come out of Washington, I'll quit my job.

"Greed for jobs, personal power, political bias too often control their better judgment.

"In the name of defense, even war or social secu-rity, the people of America must not permit this greed for power to destroy local government or the sover-eignty of the states of our representative republican system of government. It is only a step from com-plete federalized social security to taking over in the federal patronage scheme all welfare work. Then comes the United States absorbing the state highway departments. Already we hear plans for federalization of the state and local public-school systems.

"The federal government cannot encompass the whole field. It should not try. It would destroy all that we most cherish in government. We are fighting autocracy and lust for power throughout the world. Let's beat it down at home."

In Cincinnati, on October 20, Paul V. McNutt, federal social security administrator, confirmed the reports of intended federalization of unemployment compensation. The President was preparing to submit the plan to Congress, McNutt said. "It may be today, it may be tomorrow," he observed. "It has been very clearly indicated that the only way to administer unemployment insurance efficiently is on a federal basis."

Meanwhile, the federal investigation went ahead in Ohio. It was charged that Harry J. Patterson, manager of the Cincinnati employment office, had told a bureau employee where he could make a campaign contribution.

A minor employee of the Cincinnati office assumed the responsibility for the distribution of Bricker-for-Governor buttons to workers in her office, together with a memorandum from the state office of the Bureau of Unemployment Compensation stating that it was within the rights of civil-service employees to wear campaign buttons. She said that her conduct was due to her own "overzealousness in behalf of the Republicans."

Since the administrative costs of the various state bureaus of unemployment compensation are paid by the federal government, the Hatch Act was held to apply to Patterson because, it was charged, he had permitted "political activity" in his office.

The *Cincinnati Times-Star,* in an editorial entitled, "Ohio is the Whipping Boy," asserted: "We think . . . that far-sighted legislators from the other states will recognize the effort for what it is—manufactured excuse to take over one more function of state government, to the tune of $2,250,000,000, in order to enlarge the bureaucrats' happy hunting ground in Washington."

The *Bucyrus Forum* (Ohio) declared: "Governor Bricker should have the support of all Ohio in his current battle with the Roosevelt administration against encroachment upon our state rights by the proposed investigation of the Bureau of Unemployment Compensation."

The *Columbus Citizen* thought the Patterson investigation and the proposed federalization were separate issues, each of which should stand on its own feet, but, as to federalization, it said: "The Ohio delegation [in Congress] should vote as a unit against it."

"The Senators and Representatives from Ohio and other Ohio Valley states will have to answer to the people if they let this design be perpetrated," the *Cincinnati Enquirer* declared. The *Ohio State Journal* said: "They [the Roosevelt administration]

194

would like to get something on Governor Bricker. They failed in their attempt to ruin him before 1940 by trying to sell the country the idea that he was ruthlessly starving people in Cleveland. Now they are trying something else."

Even while the federal investigators were gathering their "evidence" against Patterson, other federal officials were praising him for his work. On November 6, 1941, in the thick of the investigation, Wade Hammond, Governor Bricker's appointee as director of the State Employment Service, received a letter from Colonel John N. Andrews, Re-employment Division, National Headquarters, Selective Service System, which said in part:

"It appears that you have a splendid organization for carrying out the plans of the re-employment activities, and there seems to be an excellent relationship between your good offices and those of the selective-service system.

"After speaking with you [last week], I had the opportunity of a visit with the chief of your field service, Mr. William J. Muldoon, and Colonel Harry J. Patterson, the manager of your Cincinnati office. From these conferences, it seems that there has been developed a very fine plan for carrying out the re-employment aspects of national selective service. I was happy especially to find that your several officers were so well informed on re-employment plans and that these plans were being carried out so successfully. . . ."

195

The United States Civil Service Commission ordered Patterson dismissed on a charge of violating the Hatch "clean politics" Act. It was the first application of the law anywhere in the country and some of those who had been its advocates now began to doubt its wisdom if it was to be employed in such a manner.

The charges against ten other employees of the Cincinnati employment office either were dismissed or dropped.

Of Patterson's dismissal state Bureau of Unemployment Compensation Administrator Atkinson said: "The result is exactly what anyone would expect where the investigation, prosecution, trial examination, and final decision all rested with one federal agency."

Governor Bricker announced that the Patterson case would be appealed to the federal courts; the Civil Service Commission countered with an announcement that they would reopen the case. Attorney General Herbert filed a brief with the commission on behalf of Patterson, contending that witnesses who would have refuted the charges had not been called at the hearing. "Matters of less moment have been called to the attention of the American Bar Association," remarked Herbert in his brief. The order of dismissal, he asserted, was based on "implication, inferences, and innuendo."

Within a few weeks the commission affirmed its order, effective December 15, and the state went ahead with its plans for an appeal to the federal courts. Before the fifteenth, however, the declaration of war, followed closely by federalization of employment agencies, overshadowed the case. With the State Employment Office out of existence, the state of Ohio was no longer a party in any legal dispute, so the Patterson dismissal was never passed upon by a court.

But Washington bureaucrats were still not appeased. Six weeks after his dismissal from the employment office had been ordered, Patterson had been named co-ordinator of automobile and sugar rationing in Ohio, an appointment made by the state Council of Defense, which was in charge of war rationing in its early phases. In the summer of 1942 the United States Civil Service Commission launched another investigation against Patterson, whose salary at the time was being paid by the state out of the appropriation to the Council of Defense.

As a result of that inquiry, in January 1943 the federal government held out of Ohio's unemployment-compensation funds $7,200 as a "fine" for violating the Hatch Act, on the ground that the state had employed Patterson within six weeks of his dismissal, whereas the Hatch Act forbids re-employment of persons dismissed for political activity for eighteen months.

The fine was "assessed" against the state Defense Council, although it had nothing to do with Patterson's earlier employment with the Bureau of Unemployment Compensation, and although federal funds were no longer involved in his employment. The amount of the fine was double the amount of Patterson's yearly salary as manager of the Cincinnati employment office.

Now the state was once more a party to a case involving a legal—in fact, a constitutional—question: namely, does the federal government have the power to fine a state for employing an individual whose salary is not paid by the federal government? The state of Ohio carried the case to the federal courts, where it is now pending.

In the interests of national defense, Governor Bricker acquiesced in the President's request for transfer of the state employment services to the federal government as a means of speeding up war production. But when the federal Social Security Board decided to go a step farther and demanded the federalization of the claims-taking services of the state unemployment-compensation administration, Governor Bricker wrote the President as follows:

"As governor of Ohio, I gladly agreed to your request [for the transfer of the employment service], and once more I assure you of all co-operation and that every effort will be made to assist the U.S.E.S. in the job of recruiting, training, and transferring workers for the national defense.

"I now find that the Social Security Board, despite our mutual understanding, and your Executive Order

No. 8990, plans, beginning January 1, to assume the basic state function of taking claims for unemployment insurance, an integral part of any state unemployment-compensation program.

"I cannot approve the delegation of the claims-taking operation to the United States Employment Service. I would like a response from you in regard to the return of the employment service to the state at the end of the war."

President Roosevelt had changed his views on the way in which unemployment compensation should be administered. In 1934 he had urged Congress to provide a set-up in which each state would have its own insurance system; on January 19, 1942, he was advocating a "uniform national system of insurance."

The proposal meant simply the pooling of the money paid into the federal treasury by the various states, each under its own compensation or insurance law after being collected from the employers of the respective states. In all, more than $2,000,000,000 in state taxes was involved, of which Ohio's share was $226,000,000.

The Ohio delegation in Congress, along with representatives of many other states, vigorously opposed the federalization move, and the scheme was dropped, at least temporarily. Much of the credit for halting this greatest of all attempts at centralization of power and bureaucratic expansion must go to Governor Bricker and Herschel Atkinson, the aroused public opinion in Ohio, and the opposition of the Ohio Republican delegation in Congress. Texas and Wisconsin were also leaders in the fight.

The successful stand the states made in this issue gave New Deal bureaucracy its first major setback in whittling down the sovereign rights of the states. Under the cloak of the war effort, the states might easily have fallen into the error of surrendering their powers or letting them go by default to the federal government.

Governor Bricker has taken the position that it is just as important to preserve, on the home front, the traditional freedoms guaranteed by our republican form of government as it is to win the war on the battle front; that confusing these two issues could well lead to losing the war on both fronts.

One curb on expanding bureaucracy, he has often pointed out, lies simply in a fuller assertion of its responsibility by the legislative branch of the government. He said in an address on the one-hundred-and-fiftieth anniversary of the meeting of the first Congress under the Constitution (March 1939):

"The legislative branch of government is closer to the needs of the people of our country, and must be undominated and uncontrolled by the executive branch. It must be free to reflect and to express those unselfish demands and needs of the majority of our people without transgressing upon the protected rights of the individual or minority."

In a statement issued in September 1943, he proposed another check on bureaucracy:

"If we are to continue to live under the protection of the Constitution of the United States, we must take the policy-making power of our government from the hands of arrogant bureaucrats. We must restore it to the elected representatives of the people. . . . The Constitution offers a way for curbing this growing power. I have suggested that it should be amended to limit the tenure of the President of the United States by constitutional mandate. I would favor a single term of six years. Such a step would assure the people of this country that popular government is secure, and that their basic freedom will be inviolate."

Bricker proposed that in its 1944 canvass the Republican party pledge its candidate to a single term of four years.

The Governor's crusade against expanding bureaucracy and its tightening stranglehold on the people has not been confined to the federal field. At his instance, Ohio has taken a long step toward bringing the various state license-issuing, order-issuing bureaus, departments, and agencies back to the fundamentals of democracy.

Early in his service in state government the Governor discerned the wide variations in the procedure of the various administrative agencies. Many of the laws governing the license-issuing, order-issuing agencies did not, he noted, provide for hearings relative to the granting, suspending, or revoking of li-

201

censes. In a number of instances, no judicial review of the acts of the agencies was provided; and where they were provided, there was a wide divergence on jurisdiction and procedure.

Accordingly, in 1941 he asked the legislature to establish a commission to study the situation and make recommendations to the next General Assembly. The commission found that 47 different agencies of the state government, created in the course of 131 years, were issuing 187 different types of licenses, and that a very large part of the citizens of Ohio was directly affected.

"It is a fundamental principle of the American government that a person should not be deprived of a right or privilege without a hearing if he desires one," the commission reported to the legislature; yet it had found that many of the state's licensing acts failed to provide a hearing on the revocation, suspension, refusal to issue, or refusal to renew a license. There seldom was any provision for adequate hearing, such as notice, record, and attendance of witnesses.

"There would seem to be no question but that every agency should have to offer a person a hearing," the commission went on; "and further that the hearing afforded should conform to the accepted standards of procedure for fair hearings."

The commission found a "confusing lack of uniformity on the privilege of the aggrieved person to have a decision reviewed by another tribunal."

Twenty-four of the 76 state licensing acts made no provision for any review. The commission then made detailed recommendations for consideration by the Governor and the legislature.

In January 1943 Governor Bricker said: "Administrative agencies have brought the tendency to substitute government of men for government of laws, otherwise known as bureaucracy." He asked the legislature to pass a uniform administrative-procedure act giving the citizens of Ohio the right of hearing and appeal, as well as uniformity of procedure on matters pertaining to licenses.

The legislature responded by enacting a law requiring each license-issuing agency to publish and have available for distribution at all times, all of its rules of general and uniform operation; providing a hearing for any licensee or any act of any agency regarding his license; and providing a review by the common pleas court of the agencies' decisions in regard to the licenses, the common pleas court being the court of record closest to the people.

This uniform-administrative-procedure law of Ohio is a landmark in the struggle to curb bureaucratic rule. It guarantees the processes of American government by giving every man his "day in court." It seeks to keep government close to home and to keep it responsible and responsive to the will of the people.

CHAPTER XIV

THE UNITED STATES IN THE POSTWAR WORLD

GOVERNOR BRICKER'S election to a third term immediately made him an outstanding presidential candidate whose views on national and international affairs were important to the people of the country at large. His announcement of candidacy for the nomination for President, made on November 15, 1943, declares his stand on America's collaboration in the postwar world. He said:

"There must be responsible participation by the United States in postwar co-operative organization among sovereign nations to prevent military aggression and to attain permanent peace with organized justice in a free world."

Much as a physician tries to prevent the spread of disease by quarantine, Bricker hoped that the political maladies from which Europe was suffering in 1938 and 1939 could be isolated there. When President Roosevelt called a special session of Congress on the question of repealing the arms embargo provision in the Neutrality Act, Bricker cautioned that a government's first consideration should always be the welfare of its own people.

When talk of a coalition government in this country arose after the fall of France, Bricker urged the need for a defense program that would make the United States defensible at all times against any attack; but at the same time he warned of the dangers of one-party government.

"We have seen enough of one-party government in the other parts of the world," he said. "At the present time there are such vital issues, domestic and international, that the American people ought to have a voice in determining them. I do not want to see any coalition government or cabinet parceling out jobs as between two parties which would deprive the American people of a voice in determining policy and the right to pass upon all these matters of vital concern."

A year later, when the question of using the American Navy to convoy supplies to Britain was being informally debated everywhere, Bricker deplored the President's frank avoidance of the issue in his public statements.

"The people want to know where we are going and why. They are looking to the White House for leadership. Only the President has access to the information necessary for making our decision. The people are waiting to hear from him."

He was deeply shocked by the assault on Pearl Harbor, and at once directed all state department heads, all public officials, and all citizens to direct their main energies toward defense of the nation and prosecution of the war.

In June 1943, with the biennial legislative session over and the plans for his third administration set in motion, Bricker delivered an address before the Wisconsin Bar Association in Milwaukee in which he made a brief preliminary statement on postwar collaboration among nations:

"Beyond this war lie two vital and grave decisions. Those decisions will have to be made by the American people after widespread discussion and long and serious thought. The first is, what part this nation will play in world affairs. What, in short, will be its foreign policy? The second is the question of what domestic policies this nation will adopt in fitting itself for its proper role in the world beyond the war.

"It is obvious that these two problems are intimately related. There are those who are able to discuss the one without any consideration of the other. But I cannot share such easy and complacent assurance. Whatever we promise to the world is in the nature of a promissory note. When men give promissory notes, they must, if they are honest, know how their promises can be kept. If their personal future is cloudy, if their health is infirm and their earning power doubtful, they must take that into consideration. We dare not destroy the hopes of the world because we have not been honest with ourselves.

"I join with those who wish to lend the strong arm of American help in the solution of world problems.

I find, moreover, as I meet people in all walks of life and talk with them of their fears and hopes, that they feel that the destiny of America must be, to a greater extent than before, involved in the destinies of the world at large.

"I find, in short, that people want to be shown how the United States can effectively join with other nations in solving some of the fundamental causes of war. Since that desire is so widespread and so evident, no one should ignore it. I shall never do so.

"That desire, born of the suffering of war, must be strengthened and implemented. I propose, at a time not too far removed, to speak of the possibilities of American participation in world affairs, in some detail and with some specific suggestions."

He then sounded a warning that "our position in the world depends upon policies and principles which we pursue within our borders"; recounted some of the bureaucratic attempts to implant a planned economy in the United States; and declared: "A nation which has launched itself upon a totalitarian economy cannot be the good neighbor to any other nation."

In several public statements in the spring and summer of 1943, he cautioned against "secret understandings" and "secret conferences." Repeatedly he pleaded that an opportunity for open and full debate be given on all matters, particularly those involving foreign policy. "I have an abiding confidence in the judgment of the people of our country when they know the facts," he declared in a speech in Jefferson City, Missouri.

Speaking before the National Society of the Sons of the American Revolution at Philadelphia on Constitution Day, September 17, 1943, Governor Bricker expanded his views on the peace conference that will follow the war, on postwar collaboration among the nations, and on how the decisions should be reached:

"We face a situation today which calls more eloquently than ever before for a world-wide endeavor to remove the causes of war. We must be assured that the fruits of the vast sacrifices of this war shall not be lost through lack of foresight. This assurance is a sacred obligation of the nation. This is the assurance that sacrificing American fathers and mothers are asking of those to whom they entrust leadership and office. A positive answer must be given. The answer cannot be fulfilled with words alone, even words of noble aspiration and good intent.

"To win the war, Americans will meet their tragic losses with God-given fortitude. The hour has struck when we must get beyond our good intentions and into the practical realities of our problem. What, as we face the world beyond victory, are our materials for action? Primarily we have the aid of past experience. We need more than that, but history will be a helpful guide. Many people are telling us that our past is a record of selfishness, of self-containment, and of isolation. But the facts belie that view.

208

"Ever since the alliance made with France through the offices of Benjamin Franklin at the time of the Revolution, the United States has been a world power," he said. He reviewed the repeated evidences of American participation in world affairs, such as the Monroe Doctrine, expansion of our spheres of influence following the Spanish-American War, our efforts to stabilize eastern Asia, our participation in the First World War, our contributions toward the feeding and rebuilding of Europe after that war, our participation in many international organizations for the promotion of human welfare throughout the world, our attempts to lay the foundations of peace in the Pacific, and our initiation of efforts to bring about disarmament as belying the charge of isolationism. He reiterated a statement made in New York City several months earlier: "America is not, never has been, and will never be an isolationist nation. America must deal with other nations of the world, and America must assume leadership."

The term "internationalist" is just as absurd, he declared. "No sane man would think of wiping out our national lines. That is what the United Nations are fighting to prevent."

To his Philadelphia audience, he continued: "In geographic position, in the wealth of our resources, in the ingenuity and enterprise of our people, in our potential military strength, and in the character of our government, we are the most fortunate and the strongest single nation on the face of the globe. Therefore, we have the greatest responsibility.

"If we do not, in the years following victory over the Axis powers, exert every talent, effort, and means at our command, to keep our own and other countries out of wars, then we are not worthy of our Christian heritage. . . .

"If we do not now, after the present, most destructive of all wars, make a serious and conscientious effort to build a better understanding among the nations and the peoples of the earth, then, indeed, we must stand convicted before posterity as ignorant, heartless, and unworthy reactionaries.

"The specific steps which we should take cannot at this time be detailed. No man in a position of authority has attempted so to do. The war is not yet ended. As the tide of the world battle lines advances and recedes, constantly changing governmental, economic, and living conditions arise throughout the world. No man is wise enough now to state with exactitude what this nation's obligations to others may be at the conclusion of the war, or how they may best be carried out.

"Our foreign policy should be based upon the absolute necessity for the preservation of our identity as a nation and on our traditional freedom of action at all times. Only thus can we be strong in our help of others. The United States should adhere to a policy which will preserve its constitutionalism as expressed in the Declaration of Independence, the Constitution itself, and the Bill of Rights, and as administered through our republican form of government. Constitutionalism should be adhered to in determining the substance of our policies and in the making of international commitments.

"In looking to our future foreign policy, we shall be wise to formulate carefully those plans under which our nation must live with other nations. People responsible for negotiating our foreign agreements should be truly representative of the American people. Never again should our peace negotiations be directed by those from only one political party, from any one department of government, or any one section of our national life. We do not want a one-man or one-party peace. If we believe in collaboration among the nations, we must put it in practice among Americans. . . .

"This nation must, with the other peace-seeking nations, open the door to broad co-operative efforts to build a better world. The sad ordeal of two great wars has taught us the stark reality of interdependence.

"The exact forms of co-operation among the nations are not matters to be determined in a few days. It may well be that a mere lasting peace can be achieved without a single supreme peace conference. It has been wisely suggested that many conferences may be more desirable. The making of a lasting peace may be a matter of many months or years.

"This brings me to another essential of peace-

211

making—the knowledge and consent of the American people. Consent of the governed is inherent in constitutional government. During the period in which plans for permanent collaboration are being made, there will be time for each proposal to be considered by our citizens, debated in Congress, and thoroughly examined in all its aspects. We want no treaties, this time, hastily written and thrust before us to be accepted without question. If we believe in freedom, we should act constitutionally in the spirit of freedom by showing full confidence in our own countrymen.

"Our sons," he concluded, "are offering their all in fulfillment of a sacred contract with those who shall guide our policies in the making of the peace.

"The elements of that sacred contract comprise two broad obligations. First, we must preserve the heritage of a free republic at home, strong with the treasure of free enterprise, firm in the observance of political and religious liberty, and just and humane in its attitude toward the individual. Second, this nation must, with the other peace-seeking nations of the world, open the door to broader co-operative efforts to build a better world.

"We have a covenant with our future and with our sons. That covenant can be performed only if we determine our course at home and abroad by our charter of freedom, the living declaration of faith in man's capacity to govern himself, the Constitution of the United States."

Addressing the Pennsylvania Society of New York on December 11, 1943, he said:

"Turning first to our position in the postwar world, we are encouraged by the conferences that have been held with our allies. They strengthen the war effort and assure unity of action. They set a pattern for developing mutual understanding among nations and for building an orderly peace.

"America needs a forthright foreign policy. There is nothing mysterious about foreign policy. There is no secret formula by which it can be determined. Our foreign policy should be an adaptation of far-sighted domestic policy to world relationships. Honesty, fair dealings, promises wisely made and faithfully kept, know no geographical lines and are not spoken in any one language. A sound American policy in international affairs means that we shall deal as a strong independent nation, and that other nations of the world shall deal with us on the same basis.

"Such a positive policy must be followed in the years ahead—that America's voice might be heard, our position respected, our nation defended, and our people kept proud of our position among the nations of the world. Such policy will recognize that a prosperous America requires a prosperous world. It will recognize that in rehabilitating America the rest of the world must also be rehabilitated. Peace throughout the world must be built upon the right of other people to live their lives, build their cities, replant their fields, restore their homes. All the people of the world must get down to hard work and work constructively and hopefully.

"The United States must help in every possible way to restore order and decent living throughout the world. We must do our full share in maintaining adequate instrumentalities of peace. And for these purposes, the United States will take her place in a co-operative organization among sovereign nations after this war.

"Our desires for peace must be implemented by a practical and definite program. The details will be worked out in the light of developing conditions and after full conference and open discussion. Our peace must ultimately rest upon the understanding and approval of the people of the United States. The preservation of peace is a constant and continuing obligation.

"We in America want no super-government—no dictatorial state to which we are subservient. We want no central world authority over us. Nor, do I believe, does any other sovereign nation want a central world authority over it.

"An international co-operative organization, whatever precise form it may take, can wield a tremendous influence toward peaceful solution of the international problems which have in the past led to war. These problems include trade barriers of all kinds, lack of access to raw materials, exploitation of undeveloped resources, commercial rivalries, air and water rights, especially monetary instability. Such an international organization must be founded on continuous close-working collaboration.

"This would be a long step, and it is realistic. It respects the American point of view. And it has a background of experience that shows its worth. With such a forum established, international disputes can and must be settled by arbitration and judicial decisions. When such habits of peace are formed and supported by the strong nations, we can again hope for relief from the burdens of war.

"We must move forward with the confidence that the American people will work in full co-operation with the nations of the world in the days of peace. Only in that hope and confidence can we plan or establish a just order of international relationships. A confidence in the people and their leaders in the years ahead as well as in ourselves requires that we do not attempt to place this or any other nation in an international strait-jacket. A will for peace must be transmitted by us to those who follow."

This, then, is the story of Bricker of Ohio: the man and his record. Thus he comes before the people of the United States as a candidate for President. If the story should serve as a campaign document, it is because of what the man is and because of what he has accomplished as an efficient, sound, progressive, and far-sighted administrator.